FIVE PILLARS
OF A
FIRST CLASS
LIFE

CARLA MAXWELL RAY

For inquiries, please email: contact@carlamaxwellray.com

ISBN 978-1-7330146-0-1 Paperback
ISBN 978-1-7330146-1-8 eBook

Dedication

*To my mom, Beulah Formey Maxwell, who lived a first class life,
and more importantly, helped others strive to do the same.*

*And to my grandchildren,
Kyree Nicole Ray, and Robert Anthony Ray IV
who represent our hope for the future.*

Contents

Preface:
Why I Choose Generosity

And now, as a captive to the Spirit, I am on my way. But I do not count my life of any value to myself, if only I may finish my course and the ministry that I received from the Lord Jesus, to testify to the good news of God's grace.

Acts 20:22-24 (NRSV)

My Mom's name, Beulah, which means my delight is in her. She was a genius, going to high school at nine years old and college at 13. My mother demonstrated joyful generosity throughout her life. Yes, she gave abundantly to others. Even more generous was her treatment of others and her graciousness—no judgement, yet she always brought high expectations. Mom pushed us all to be our personal best.

For instance, there was a single mom of eight children at our church. Mom would very discretely slip her money nearly every time they saw each other. And how do I know? Only because my Dad told me when all three were in their eighties.

As I matured, I became a professional fundraiser, helping various esteemed institutions raise over one billion dollars. From my experiences, I was fortunate to spend quality time with wealthy and generous individuals. I witnessed, firsthand and up close, their lifestyles and their *why* for living.

In fact, I define my career as one who helps others to live their God-ordained purpose. I also help them to fund their passions.

Consistently, these high-capacity families and individuals exhibited what I call *the five pillars of a First Class life.*

I've had the privilege of personally experiencing and observing pastors, Nobel Laureates, CEOs of Fortune 500 companies, celebrities, and regular folk—all of whom give generously to help a vision become reality. As we read in Scripture:

Many people have set out to write accounts about the events that have been fulfilled among us. They used the eyewitness reports circulating among us from the early disciples. Having carefully investigated everything from the beginning, I also have decided to write an accurate account for you, most honorable Theophilus, so you can be certain of the truth of everything you were taught.

Luke 1:1-4 (NLT)

Like Luke, who wrote to his friend Theophilus, I've set out to write my account for you. I want to share with you what I have learned so you can be, as Luke says, "certain of the truth."

That's what my life is all about—sharing the good things that have come to me. I want to leave this world empty of all God has given me, just like my dear mom, Beulah Maxwell. Because when you do what God purposes, you never work a day in your life.

Instead, you enjoy fulfilling your destiny and purpose.

For we are God's handiwork, created in Christ Jesus to do good works, which God prepared in advance for us to do.

Ephesians 2:10 (NIV)

How this Book Came to Be

Generis (www.generis.com) is a Christian firm dedicated to accelerating generosity to fund God-inspired vision. There I coach churches and nonprofits. One day, one of my clients expressed frustration about the lack of a good resource for generous, fiscally responsible living.

While taking a ride on a train after that client visit, I reflected. I had a *Eureka* moment—I felt God preparing me to fill that void; to write a book about true, First Class life. It wasn't a "one moment" feeling, but the impression that he'd been preparing me *all* my life to do this.

This book responds to the needs of families and individuals to be fiscally free to pursue their purpose in life. As an expert in biblical stewardship- teaching, generosity consulting, and mission-driven living, I discovered all three of these are interrelated. When the three are linked, they become the cornerstone of living a First Class life.

I created Five Pillars to guide you through creating a mission statement for your life so that you too can begin fulfilling your destiny and purpose. Throughout the book, there are Scripture verses and passages to serve as guiding principles for you, with additional readings at the back of the book. However, this book is for everyone who is open to learning a healthy life and fiscal lessons. In these pages, I open up and share specific circumstances and experiences that helped me mature and live a more abundant life.

Acknowledgments

I'm grateful for all of those who helped me bring this book to life:

Lord and Savior, Jesus Christ, who planted this idea within me, prepared me my entire life for such writing and sent me the teachers to help me along the way

Husband, Rev. Robert A. Ray, the love of my life and my Pastor

Dad, Troy Maxwell, who gave me my foundation to work hard, save much, and positively impact my sphere of influence

Children and their spouses who keep me relevant and show me, consistent love

Sisters, Rev. Angela Maxwell Brown and my twin, Carmen T. Maxwell, who keep me humble and inspire me

Clients, who I partner with to grow generosity in their church and nonprofits

Coach, Linda Griffin, whose expertise guided my book

Editor, Robert Suggs, who gave my book the lift it needed

Mentor, Valerie Tripp, who gave unselfishly of her time and literary expertise

Beta readers: Val Traore, Justin Brown and Don Martin

Generis Strategists for your bold and innovative approach to enhancing generosity, in particular, CEO Jim Sheppard and President Brad Leeper. Special accolades to Vice President Dr. Herman Norman, who introduced me to generosity some 20 years ago.

AME and AME Zion Church that keeps me spiritually grounded, especially my local church, Bishop and Supervisor Davis, and Bishop and Supervisor Proctor

Introduction

I'm a journal-keeper. It is a consistent practice I highly recommend. Over time, I've found it to be an amazing help in organizing my life and my thoughts. I've collected a number of my journal entries here because I feel they will provide the best guidepost for you and your family as you create that mission statement toward a First Class life.

I've organized my thoughts into five pillars:

1. *Be Disciplined.*
2. *Be a Masterpiece.*
3. *Be Radically Generous.*
4. *Be Diligent.*
5. *Be Resilient.*

Within each pillar, you'll find reflections based on my personal experience, as well as interesting facts and thought-provoking questions to help you define, fund, and above all, live a First Class life.

Following each reflection are questions to help you answer your why in preparation for creating your personal mission statement. Please use a composition book or journal (if you're "old school") or an online file/folder (if you're "new school") to answer the discussion questions, so you can easily keep track and reference them.

Among the questions are Scripture passages that directly relate to your mission statement. Read the verses and reflections, then answer the questions. Write the answers, so they include the question subject.

For example:

✓ Question: What impact do I want to have?

✓ Answer: I will impact people's lives by helping them to live fiscally healthy lives.

The answers you provide will become the input to your personal mission statement and will define:

ↄ What you are purposed to do.

ↄ How you will uncover and fulfill that purpose.

ↄ What you need to be fiscally prepared to embark upon that journey.

ↄ How what you are purposed to do will drive your actions.

When you have completed the book and answered all the questions, you'll be ready to write your First Class life mission statement.

Let's agree on an important point: A First Class life is not a position you strive to achieve. Instead, it's a dynamic process that never ends; a lifestyle you choose daily.

Here's my mission statement about which you may hold me accountable:

My goal in life is to glorify God by using my gifts for seeing possibilities and empowering others to achieve, advance, and fund their vision for their lives and/or organizations. My passions for innovation, finance, and healthy living positively impact my family, the Christian community, and all those I encounter. I value wisdom, excellence, generosity, and self-discipline.

Note: To all English Teachers including my mom:

First Class or First-Class? Yes according to Webster, First Class is a noun and First-Class is an adjective. Technically, I should use first-class. I ask you to pardon my grammar in advance as I take literary license and do what 'feels' best.

Setting the Stage for Living a First Class Life

A First Class Life True Story

Pastor had always wanted to sit in First Class—just once. So, he bought a ticket for his next flight.

After boarding first, he was now settling in. Just as he was about to order, an old friend, Sean, boarded with the coach passengers. They hadn't seen each other in more than a decade. They shook hands, exchanged cards, and promised to catch up. Seeing other coach passengers behind him, Sean headed quickly to coach seating.

A couple of weeks later, another associate asked Pastor if he'd heard the news about their friend Sean. Pastor said they'd recently spoken on a plane. The news was that Sean had recently sold his company for tens of millions to a Fortune 500 company. Pastor realized his old friend was living a First Class life while riding in coach.

The pastor is my husband.

I looked at him and said, "You may be in First Class on Delta. I'll sit next to Sean in coach and live a First Class life."

Scripture tells us how to do that. It's a life of grace, harvest, and overflow.

Remember this: Whoever sows sparingly will also reap sparingly, and whoever sows generously will also reap generously. Each man should give what he has decided in his heart to give, not reluctantly or under compulsion, for God loves a cheerful giver. And God is able to make all grace abound to you, so that in all things at all times, having all that you need, you will abound in every good work. As it is written:

"He has scattered abroad his gifts to the poor; his righteousness endures forever."

Now he who supplies seed to the sower and bread for food will also supply and increase your store of seed and will enlarge the harvest of your righteousness. You will be made rich in every way so that you can be generous on every occasion, and through us your generosity will result in thanksgiving to God.

2 Corinthians 9:6-11

Sowing Generously

An Essential First Class Life Component:
Lifestyle Stewardship*[3]

Lifestyle Stewardship will elevate your life to new levels of generosity and fulfillment.

He who loves pleasure will become poor; whoever loves wine and oil will never be rich.

Proverbs 21:17

Lifestyle stewardship*[1] is a concept adapted from my work at Generis, based on 2 Samuel 24:24. I will not offer God that which costs me nothing. There are three steps:

Step 1: Reassess Your Lifestyle.

An honest appraisal of our material wealth. "Be sure you know the condition of your flock; give careful attention to your herds" (Proverbs 27:23).

Do you know the impact of the new tax laws on your finances?

Do you keep track of the ebb and flow of the stock market?

How about your house value?

What factors in the economy will impact you, and how are you adjusting for those changes?

Step 2: Reorder Your Priorities.

We need a conscientious appraisal of our values. "In the same way, any of you who does not give up everything he has, cannot be my disciple" (Luke 14:33).

---

3   Generis
1   Generis

Look at your online accounts, checking, credit cards, and others. What do they reveal about your priorities?

Step 3: Reallocation of Resources.

This is a serious consideration of where we want to invest ourselves. "Therefore, if you are not faithful in the use of worldly wealth, who will entrust true riches to you?" (Luke 16:11).

Take action and be a good, trusted steward over what you do have.

Biblical stewardship is not about what God wants from you, but what God wants for you.

The desire of the righteous ends only in good, but the hope of the wicked only in wrath.

One man gives freely, yet gains even more; another withholds unduly, but comes to poverty.

A generous man will prosper; he who refreshes others will himself be refreshed.

Proverbs 11:23-25

Numbers Reveal the Truth

I'm pleased you're embarking on a journey of discovery about your real self and how money impacts you. Often, you hear the expression that numbers cannot lie—they offer a true reflection of who we are, our priorities and our hearts. "Where your treasure is, there is your heart also." Matthew 6:21.

In later sections, you'll examine where your money goes. You'll decide if you overextend yourself fiscally because of habit, impulsive desires, or to impress. Many of us consume way more than we should.

Still others are selfish and hold onto the little they have. Generosity is not only reserved for the wealthy and the well-endowed. Even those of us who have little can experience generous, full lives.

This book is a guide to help you accomplish generously what you can and in your places of opportunity.

The Cardinal: Symbol of Living a First Class Life

 That beautiful red bird, the cardinal, is symbolic of power, wealth, and enthusiasm. Knowing what you want and how to get it: This is the central power of the cardinal.

That may seem odd to you: How did the cardinal of all creatures become a symbol of a First Class life? Let me tell you a little story.

A few years ago, my husband and I ate lunch at a cafe. We sat at a window, finishing our meal while discussing our life and blessings together. Outside the window, a beautiful cardinal landed. He focused in on us as if to deliver a message. My husband had an intuitive feeling that the arrival of a cardinal symbolized good news for us.

We believe in the power of a personal symbol, something visual that carries meaning and inspiration.

After researching this bird, I understood what he represented and how that aligned with our lives. Cardinals are strong, beautiful, assertive, and there's even a recent report that shows they suppress certain infections, such as the West Nile virus. What a fascinating creation of God is this lovely bird.

Whenever you see a cardinal symbol beside a question in the remainder of this book, it will identify those questions that directly correspond to writing your life mission statement. In the meantime, think about a symbol you'd like to use to represent your life. Be specific, write down what you want, research, and have some fun finding a symbol to reflect your desire.

The First Class Life Equation for Success

Time for an equation. Don't worry, no real math is involved!

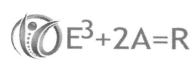 $E^3+2A=R$ **Empower** (cubed) (by Equipping, Educating and Encouraging **plus 2A** (Actions times Accountability) **equals Results** (competence, fiscal prowess, and spiritual growth).

I'm often asked what I do to help Christian organizations, churches, and their leaders realize their vision. I explain it in an "algebraic" style of equation. The Lord revealed to me that the Es have an exponential relationship. That is, they don't simply add to each other—they multiply each other for a powerful, vast result. In numbers, if you had 10 plus 15, you come up with only 15. But if you multiply them by each other, the result is 150. That's the power of exponential process.

Empower and build teams by equipping them with tools and biblical principles. Educate as to best practices and customized strategies. Encourage to stay the course and keep everyone's eyes on the prize.

As I coach the leadership team through the process, I help people uncover unexplored talents and capabilities. Specifically, I share tools that are customized for the church or nonprofit organization (NPO).

And even more significantly, I coach them through strategies that enhance and make their efforts more effective. Still, the hard work must be done to create a culture of generosity in a church or NPO. This coaching is done through Generis, a top Christian firm that accelerates generosity for God-inspired vision.

One strategy is to coach the pastor or CEO through conversations with high-capacity donors. God endows our churches with members and NPOs with supporters who have various talents. Yet many ignore the gift of wealth. Or worse yet, they don't address disobedience in stewardship and the increasing debt among their members. Both ends of the spectrum will smother the resources needed to actualize their vision.

The two As (action and accountability) have a multiplicity relationship in that they partner as twins—twice the impact when actions are coupled with accountability. This means tasks with deadlines, follow up, reporting, milestones, etc. A lack of accountability is among the top reasons that churches and NPOs fail in executing plans. That goes for you and me, too.

The reason I do this work is the sustainable transforming change in givers' lives. This defines the R, which results in team competence, spiritual growth and money for God-inspired vision. When we realize everything belongs to God (1 Chronicles 29:11-12), we are set free. Giving is for the believer.

God gave me this algebraic formula when I started generosity coaching to help to define my coaching quantitatively. If you created an algebraic expression for your life's work, what would it be? What is your equation for success?

First Class Life Economic Fact:

To Become More Philanthropic, Shift to Thrift

Adapted from Consumer Spending Trends and Current Statistics by Kimberly Amadeo.

Consumer spending, a major economic indicator, totals almost $14 trillion and is 68 percent of the U.S. economy. As consumers, we buy services, such as housing and healthcare; non-durable goods, such as clothing and groceries; and other items, such as automobiles and appliances.

Strong consumer spending is the main reason the Gross Domestic Product growth remains healthy. The Bureau of Labor Statistics reports that the average American spent $57,311 in 2016.

Average annual expenditures and characteristics of all consumer units, Consumer Expenditure Survey, 2013-2017

Item	2013	2014	2015	2016	2017
Number of consumer units (in thousands)	125,670	127,006	128,437	129,549	130,001
Consumer unit characteristics					
Income before taxes	$63,784	$66,877	$69,627	$74,664	$73,573
Income after taxes	$56,352	$58,364	$60,448	$64,175	$63,606
Average annual expenditure	$51,110	$53,495	$55,978	$57,311	$60,060

Source: Consumer Expenditure Survey, U.S. Bureau of Labor Statistics, September, 2018.

It took a while for consumer spending to bounce back. Why?

First, many discovered new job paths by educating themselves in lucrative careers. School loans increased significantly, with auto loans comprising the greatest percentage of consumer debt. Credit card debt is shrinking. Hopefully, some lessons were learned about paying for something as you acquire it.

Second, with globally outsourced jobs, income levels are behind. The result is an increase in savings, less spending, and depressed consumer confidence.

Third, the demand for lower-cost, high-value products and services are also due to technology accessibility and efficiencies. The Internet allows shoppers to search for more for less.

After the recession, the consumer remained frugal and didn't return to the full-price model. The "keeping up with the Joneses" mentality has been blown up. Remember the subprime mortgage crisis, when home equity loans were considered easy cash? Credit card balances were staggering. The wakeup call worked as many lost their secure jobs.

To become more philanthropic, my husband and I shifted our consumer spending to thrift. We looked for quality items and services we valued and/or needed. Then we researched and searched for buying options that gave us the same quality for as little as ten cents on the dollar.

With patience and resisting the trends, we have been shockingly successful. From estate sales, online auctions, buy/sell apps, and websites, to bartering—we have acquired higher quality items for much less. Our only regret is not doing this sooner.

In order to live a First Class life and become debt free, begin to adjust your lifestyle and spending habits, not only when the economic forecast calls for a recession but in healthy economic seasons as well.

Pillar 1: Be Disciplined

They disciplined us for a little while as they thought best; but God disciplines us for our good, in order that we may share in his holiness. No discipline seems pleasant at the time, but painful. Later on, however, it produces a harvest of righteousness and peace for those who have been trained by it.

Hebrews 12:10-11

The "D" Word!

Nobody is a fan, really. When we hear the word, it means keeping our children in line; watching our figure; getting up early to exercise— all kinds of inconveniences!

Yet nearly everything good in your life has been the result of some kind of discipline. You had to do chores to get your allowance, and you had to study to make good grades. You had to learn what it meant to work hard for a full day. Discipline is God's factory for strong character. It's not only how things are done but how we become the people he wants us to be.

And the truth of discipline very much applies when it comes to our finances.

In this pillar, you will think about:

- ⊃ How you plan to change your spending to enhance relationships.
- ⊃ What changes in your lifestyle you can make to better reflect your gratitude for what you already have?
- ⊃ What is impeding you from being fiscally healthy and secure?
- ⊃ How you will embark upon a journey of fiscal freedom.

DEFINE YOUR MISSION

Reflection: Wisdom Paired with Money

Wisdom is better when it's paired with money, especially if you get both while you are still living. Double protection: wisdom and wealth! Plus, this bonus: Wisdom energizes its owner.

Ecclesiastes 7:11 (The Message)

Above all other things, seek wisdom for it will enable you to accomplish much. However, God does instruct us that as we acquire money, be wise in its use. Long term, we want to achieve sustainable wealth that will be used to help us fulfill our purpose and help others. New levels of resourcing help us to apply wisdom more broadly and effectively.

Some of the richest people lack wisdom—that is, understanding and knowledge. They respond out of emotion, ego, pride, selfishness, and trends. Look at many of our celebrities and political figures; some are obnoxious and immature, yet they are rich.

In my profession, I know many rich people. Still, I was blessed to be raised by parents of high wisdom and resources. My mother, Beulah Maxwell, spent her early years with a chicken coop as her home. Her community, Leland, NC, limited the education of African Americans to eighth grade. So, my mom was sent to the 'big city,' Wilmington, NC, to attend high school at nine years old. She lived with her Principal and took care of her baby. My mom graduated from high school and enrolled in college at 13 years old. My father, Troy Maxwell, grew up on a farm in one of the most economically depressed counties in the nation, Lane, Williamsburg County, SC. My Dad's family owned their land, and it produced much for their needs. Dad went to live with his grandmother when he was young because her husband had passed and she needed help. As a result, my Dad had to drop out of school. His grand-mother was not educated. Despite the lack of education, my Dad acquired several rental properties and grew his portfolio of assets over time. Rev. Dr. Al Hathaway, the son of one of my Dad's best friends, said, Troy mentored me and was one of my living examples of the three principles of economics:

M1 - a person works a job for money
M2 - people work for you and you make money
M3 - your money works for you and makes money.

Dad, who eventually returned to school as an adult, used his leadership skills in the community, at church and at work. Yet despite their start, my parents lived wise lives and built wealth. They were able to increase their resources steadily.

Questions to Answer:

- Write about someone you know who is both wealthy and wise.
- What will you do to increase your wisdom so that when wealth comes, you can handle it?
- List three things that impede wealth.

Reflection: Time is a Gift From God

Take the Time: Order my house, then set a vision.

In so many ways, time is the ultimate resource. And God pays every single one of us in the exact same amount: twenty-four hours for each day! How are we going to invest that payment?

When was the last time you spent time studying your use of time? Maybe it's high time!

Lord, I trust you to keep our household and family. Thank you for the time to:

Reflect
Love
Organize
Study
Maximize our investments
Build our business
Lead your people
Exercise
Eat healthily
Hug frequently
Mentor
Optimize my time
Seize the moment and appreciate it

Questions to Answer:

⊃ What is your vision for your life?

⊃ How will you reprioritize and take the time to reorder your house to align with the vision you have for your life?

⊃ Make a commitment to five steps to better utilize your time.

Reflection: Go Out into the Deep

God has directed me to go deeper. I likewise challenge you. This involves narrowing your scope, focusing on a few, being selective, high quality versus quantity, preparing the ground before launching, pursuing excellence, fulfillment and full attention.

Luke 5 shows how God wants us to go deeper in the Lord—into Him.

He wants us to see miracles and to trust him more.

Don't tell it all; let others report. Though nothing may happen at first, keep on, and your efforts will make a huge difference.

To fulfill my life purpose, here are five steps I need to do:

- Reflect—meditate and be quiet.
- Trust—that I am on a path directed by God that will result in glorification to his kingdom and in my good.
- Listen—for unsaid things. Keep my eyes open, respond to my heart, think through implications.
- Discern—look and see what is really going on.
- Act—be courageous!

Luke 5 shows us how Jesus asked Simon (later called Peter) to pull away from the crowd. Simon and others are fishing in their boats with nets when Jesus teaches several *pull away from the crowd* life-altering lessons. Read the story, and then think about these points:

Lesson 1: Luke 5:3. God asks us to pull away from the crowd; leave our secure place; separate ourselves; look to Christ for instructions.

Lesson 2: Luke 5:3-4. Have the tools in hand and ready for use. Go deep, then anticipate a catch.

Lesson 3: Luke 5:5. Sometimes, we may work hard and do our best without results. Follow Christ's instructions, even though it may seem redundant or fail to make sense. Shallow attempts produce little. "Call to me and I will answer. I will tell you marvelous and wonderous things that you could never figure out on your own" (Jeremiah 33:2-3, The Message).

Lesson 4: Luke 5:6. Do what God instructs. Again, go deep and see the results.

Lesson 5: Luke 5:7. Get help with handling the abundance. Have partners, and everyone will benefit.

Lesson 6: Luke 5:8. Prepare for more than enough!

Questions to Answer:

ᴐ What six steps will you take to go deeper?

ᴐ How will your life become more fulfilling by going deeper?

ᴐ Seek an accountability partner. Write out who it may be.

FUND YOUR MISSION

Reflection: Black Friday Helps Puts America in the Red

The headline blared, "U.S. Household Debt Sets Record High."

As we embarked upon Black Friday—the top shopping day of the year—our household debt reached an all-time high. What an irony that we spend on things that don't matter. Where are our priorities? Smiles at Christmas or long-term fiscal health?

Make spending decisions that show you care versus giving the latest trendy gift. You choose!

As I write these words, total consumer debt exceeds $13.5 trillion, breaking all records. A major indicator that the economy may slow down is the rise in student delinquencies. Still, mortgages are driving this high debt. Meanwhile, with low unemployment, the economy continues to grow. In fact, if growth continues until next year, it will represent the longest period of growth ever.

So, the news is both good and bad: low unemployment (good!) and record high debt (not good at all). How all of this affects your own life will vary depending on several factors, including your income, security, and the amount of non-appreciating debt you have.

Black Friday is an opportunity to save on key, planned purchases that you can afford. Exercising discipline and self-control are essential before indulging. As for me, I feel the strong temptations of attractive sales items, and I over-purchase. Maybe you're the same way.

Target what you need and have already budgeted. Don't get caught up in the hype.

Remember, Thanksgiving is about being grateful for what we do have. Spend time with family instead of on stuff. These experiences will last a lifetime.

Questions to Answer:

⊃ Do you shop on Black Friday?

⊃ How will you change your spending to enhance relationships?

⊃ What changes in your lifestyle can you make to better reflect your gratitude for what you do have?

⊃ List three changes and post them where you (and others) may see them.

Reflection: Focus on What You Do Have

Frequently in life, we look around for something more, at what we lack, and we give in to our insatiable desire for more, more, more. It's not that we don't have enough; it's our focus on what we don't have instead of what we do.

It's much healthier to live a life of gratitude, celebrating the gifts in hand. Take a survey of your possessions. If you were to separate what you need from what you want, you would see the abundance in your life.

Those who choose to live with less, live less complex and more joyful lives. Put your focus on the abundance you enjoy. Take excellent care of your possessions and strive to enjoy them now rather than looking to what's next and what might seem better or trendier.

The disciples came to Jesus with a problem. How were they to feed 5,000 people?

Jesus challenged them to look around and gather what they had. They received five loaves of bread and two fish from a young boy who was willing to share all that he had. Jesus blessed the food, and it was more than enough, as 5,000 people were fed. (Mark 6:35-44)

Questions to Answer:

‣ Write a list of the top 20 items you own, including accounts, property, values, and funds, and write down the value of each item.

‣ Star (*) ten items/funds you are grateful to have.

‣ Is it possible you may give something of value to others?

‣ What are you able to share and ask God to bless?

Reflection: Advanced Commitment

A young man stood on his feet to share his journey with a gathering. He had just started his career. His job was sufficient to cover his living expenses; still, he had significant debt through student loans.

As he was reflecting on how to overcome his situation, he had an epiphany.

He took out his checkbook and wrote a check to God. The amount equaled his weekly pay. He told God he wanted this to be his weekly giving, not his weekly pay. He believed that was the right way to act in faith before God. The young man began giving consistently and generously to his church.

Some years later, this young man shared a copy of the check written to God. His giving now exceeds that check, and he does it online. Still, his advanced commitment to God propelled his income to a significant level.

People make advanced commitments frequently. Whether it's when we become engaged to be married or put a deposit on a home, we consider it par for the course. Yet God, our ultimate provider, is a much lower priority for us. Why is that?

Questions to Answer:

⊃ Write about a time when you made a significant commitment in advance, based on trust and confidence.

⊃ What are your financial priorities?

Reflection: "Do You Really Want to be Healed?"

My husband and I stopped by Boston Market to pick up supper. As we paid for our meals, my husband nudged me. He looked toward a panhandler who was eating in the dining area.

I recognized him as the panhandler who stood on our neighborhood corner, collecting money every weekday from cars stopping for the red light.

The panhandler was smiling and slowly counting a large roll of money, consisting of several twenties, tens, and five-dollar bills. As I searched through my purse for my smartphone to video the man, he noticed the stares and quickly gathered himself, tucked away his money, and returned to the corner.

John 5 tells the story of a disabled man who sat by a pool thought to have healing powers. For 38 years, somehow, he never made it into those waters. Jesus asked him if he wanted to be made whole. He said no one had helped him. Do you think he might have found a helper in nearly four decades if he'd earnestly wanted that?

I thought of this question when I saw the man counting his money. I don't know the panhandler's background or how he ended up in this situation. He does seem to treat begging as a regular job. I was astonished about the amount of cash he possessed. Still, could he be gainfully employed? Are there human service agencies that may usher him towards sustainability and independence?

Then I thought about this question for all of us, not just one man on a street corner. What do we really want?

Our finances are a reflection of who we are.

John 5:3 lists different adjectives indicative of disabilities: blind, sick, withered, and paralyzed. Our finances are a reflection of who we are. Our fiscal health reflects symptoms such as:

⊃ Physical or mental disability;
⊃ Bondage through debt, which is slavery;
⊃ Lack of prioritizing through excessive consumption;

⊃ Immaturity and impatience through worshiping the "now" lifestyle;
⊃ Dissatisfaction through greediness;
⊃ Selfishness through ego-driven decision-making and spending;
⊃ Paralysis by past hurts and disappointments;
⊃ Laziness, deception, ignorance, and undisciplined lives.

With faith, we can gain strength and move forward. Think differently and be open, be prayerful, and be bold. As Jesus said on another occasion, take up your mat and walk! God cures us of our disabilities, and our finances will be strong as a result.

Questions to Answer:

⊃ What is your infirmity?

⊃ How does it affect your finances?

⊃ How do we join our resources and energy together to serve others and show a better way?

Reflection: Count the Cost

The face value of a fiscal expenditure doesn't reveal the actual cost.

Years ago, I attended the wedding and reception of my childhood friend. My husband and I were a young couple just starting our family. We depended on my husband's meager yet sufficient income, and things were tight. Yet we were content. I could pause for a season and be at home with our young children.

My childhood friend was about to marry. She was important to me, and I celebrated her marriage. We decided to give the newly married couple a sacrificial gift. This money was designated for another activity. Still, I wanted to leave an impression and tangibly show our love.

Months later, I had not heard from my childhood friend. Not even a thank you.

Perhaps next time, I should count the cost, consider the sacrifice, and give what I could afford (not what I wished to give).

Questions to Answer:

꩜ Have you ever given too much for your budget? Why did you do this?

꩜ How can you avoid doing this in the future?

꩜ Would the person value the gift as much as the sacrifice?

Reflection: Shedding Light and Love in Dark Places

God has called us to go into places of darkness and evil, of discontent and disobedience, and bring his light and love there.

Financial promiscuity is a symptom of an undisciplined people who do not know God's way, or who choose not to follow it.

Financial promiscuity is a symptom of an undisciplined people

Jesus is the light and the Way, and to follow him is to prosper. (See John 8.)

Jesus is the light of the world so that whoever follows him will not walk in darkness but will have the light of life.

One of the reasons I write is to enlighten my readers on how to live a life free of the burden of financial slavery. Not only that, but God promises us a life that prospers when we live by certain spiritual fiscal promises.

Frankly, these principles don't make sense by any ordinary human standard. They involve generosity instead of hoarding, trusting in God instead of being cynical and self-driven. Still, every day I meet people who embark on this journey of faith. In every case, I find they're flourishing as a result.

Questions to Answer:

- ⊃ Are you willing to embark upon a journey of fiscal freedom?
- ⊃ How will you start?
- ⊃ Commit to a new way for 30 days and see what happens.

Reflection: Buy Once!*

Before making a purchase, ask yourself these questions. You may find them difficult; they may step on your toes; they may not be the kinds of things you want to think about. But these are the questions fiscally wise people ask themselves every day.

- ꞔ Is this something I'll pass on to my grandchild?
- ꞔ Is this a temporary need?
- ꞔ Can I make do with what I have?
- ꞔ Do I absolutely love it? (My best friend would always challenge me with this question when we went shopping)
- ꞔ Will I use it?
- ꞔ Is it the quality I deserve?
- ꞔ What else could I do with this money that would positively impact my finances and quality of life?
- ꞔ Will this last, and does the manufacturer stand behind it?

You may repurpose, recycle, and/or revamp that special item. Try sites such as Buymeonce.com that help us find sustainable, durable products so that we might purchase wisely.

As you plan purchases, ask yourself the above key questions.

Question to Answer:

- ꞔ What have you bought once and it was a wise purchase?

Reflection: Create a Strong Foundation

If your foundation is not strong, it may collapse during times of stress, pressure, or extra weight.

My dog and I had surgery, and we were sitting, recovering, and home alone. We were enjoying reading a book and peacefully bonding. Everything seemed to have gone very well—until . . .

The cabinets from the kitchen wall collapsed and fell to the floor, destroying 75 percent of the dishes contained in the cabinet.

You see, we'd just moved into this home, and the former homeowners had redone the kitchen. Obviously, they used a contractor who had limited experience in hanging and installing cabinets. In addition, the cabinets were made out of plywood—substandard materials.

My dog and I jumped! We were frightened by the thunderous sound and literally shaking. Then we went into the kitchen to inspect what had occurred. We had no idea what had caused that awful commotion.

The damage was massive. Most of the cabinets had fallen and broken mostly everything inside. I called our home owner's insurance and gathered kitchen contractors' quotes. Instead of crying over the loss (many of the broken pieces were treasured wedding gifts), I focused on designing our new kitchen. As you can imagine, the cleanup was tedious and difficult with one healthy arm.

Still, what a fun process to create my new kitchen from scratch!

Later, it happened again—this time with our closet. Poor construction resulted in a weak foundation, not strong enough to handle the pressure of over-consumption.

Cabinet catastrophe. Closet clamor. These are symbols of what we see happening in our buy-crazy world, with our substandard, poorly constructed consumer habits.

Questions to Answer:

- ⊃ Does your budget have a strong foundation?
- ⊃ Is it built on biblical principles of fiscal accountability?
- ⊃ Do you have spending habits that may result in stress on your current fiscal situation?
- ⊃ What preventive mechanisms are in place, such as insurance, auto savings plans, and retirement auto savings?

Reflection: UNAWARE

Are we truly #UNAWARE? Allen Stone wrote and sung this song about the United States' economic status. How unaware we are of what fiscally goes on in our country. Yes, it is difficult to keep up with the new tax laws, the Euro currency value impact on the dollar, and our own growing list of expenditures.

Wake up and be fiscally aware!

Some of us take better care of our cars then our finances. We get full inspections, engine checkups, tire rotations, and we keep the car spick and span. That's great. But what about your finances, which make everything in your daily life possible? Are they any less important?

Your finances need the equivalent of your automobile's regular oil change and full maintenance.

Questions to Answer:

- Are you aware of our national economy and its impact on your finances and life?
- Make a commitment to measure, at least on a monthly basis, your progress. Plan and adjust.
- Put your financial review day on your calendar monthly.

To find out more about debt today, go to: https://www.thebalance.com/consumer-debt-statistics-causes-and-impact-3305704.

LIVE YOUR MISSION

Reflection: The Morning Run

Everyone knows that we should rise early in the morning and go for a run. Why don't we do that?

To start a day off right and be more productive, to have long term health and wellness, we exercise early and first. Priorities. Urgent before optional. First things first—right?

Study those who are wise, happy, and successful in life. You'll find that they've decided what's important, attacked those tasks first, and cut out everything that doesn't matter.

Prayer is another example. What could be more critical? It's the spiritual version of a nice morning run. Stretch your prayer muscles. Start on your knees, asking God for guidance and protection. Meditate on his promises.

The road to life is a disciplined life; ignore correction and you're lost for good.

Proverbs 10:17 (The Message)

We must develop the discipline, stamina, and dogma to handle first things first. And finances are among the things of first importance in our lives. They require discipline and planning. That is how we end up on top!

Questions to Answer:

つ Why don't you do what you must and/or should?

つ List the top three obstacles in your way?

つ Examine your priorities and rearrange them to be a better you. Write down what you will do differently.

Reflection: First Things First

Relationships

- ⊃ Love First
- ⊃ Business second
- ⊃ Systems third

I had to leave my position, and I felt the pain we all feel over such a loss. Then, on my last day on the job, the team called me and expressed love and admiration. The support and concern of my friends meant so much. It healed me from the hurt of my departure.

When we look at life and all it has to offer, reflecting on the times that are most significant, love is at the center. I'm not only speaking about a wedding day or a birth—just the everyday occurrences where we may offer support and encouragement.

This has been my greatest flaw in the past. Being an achiever, occasionally I focus on the goal and obtaining the prize.

what is truly important—love

Still, I often remind myself of what is truly important—love. Who would we be without the people we care deepest about?

Questions to Answer:

- ⊃ How do you express love?
- ⊃ What might you do to increase quality time and love with those most important to you?

Reflection: Maturity

The Bible tells us that every time there is a season under heaven. Every age and stage of life has something unique and beautiful about it so that the journey is never dull. Have you ever noticed?

20 is the age of growing.
30 is the age of learning.
40 is the age of adulthood.
50 is the age of maturity.
60 is the age of comfort.
70 is the age of blessing.
80 is the age of wisdom.
90 is the age of holiness.
100 is the age of perfection.

relate multi-generationally

When we relate multi-generationally, we realize where we are, where we used to be, and where we must go. The decades of life do not define our station nor our maturity. There are blurred lines between all ages, yet we hope to advance and mature as we age. My Dad will be 90 years young, and my grandson will be one year. I'm sandwiched somewhere in between. I learn from both – the joy of discovery and the comfort of reflection.

Appreciating the diversity of each stage in life will enable us to propel ourselves to new levels of impact.

Questions to Answer:

⊃ How do you handle generational differences?
⊃ What have you learned from those of a different era?

Reflection: Marie Kondo's method of Tidying Up

The Netflix show Tidying Up is a fascinating series in the makeover genre, showing us how to declutter the stuff that takes up space and prohibits us from being our best. It will change the way you view your abode!

Before organizing, you must declutter. This is true not only of your home but with your entire life. In particular, decluttering is a fabulous idea when it comes to your finances.

Before organizing, you must declutter

But how do we tidy up our finances?

The following steps are patterned after Marie Kondo's philosophy of "tidying up."

1. Reflect/Meditate/Pray.

We give thanks and express gratitude for all that we have. We acknowledge the privilege of being the manager of numerous resources including money, possessions, and assets. We seek guidance as we disseminate and dispense of our possessions and resources.

2. Confess.

We confess our inabilities and mistakes while acknowledging our desire to become wiser and more resourceful.

3. Start with the obvious.

With finances, we all have areas that tempt us more than others. Purchasing clothing for some, while eating out and/or entertainment are sources of waste and impulsive spending. Some swipe their debit or credit cards excessively and need to pray or meditate before making expenditures. Ask yourself why. Deal with the key reasons and stop.

4. Downsize your credit cards.

Use one card that you pay off monthly. Preferably use the card for emergencies. Yes, I understand credit cards have perks and rewards. You need them for online and mobile app purchases such as Uber, hotels, and subscriptions. Still, the trap for some is undisciplined spending and perceived accessibility to funds they don't have. This is a great place to start decluttering.

5. Establish an Emergency Fund.

I bet you've heard this a million times—"saving for a rainy day." Yet the threat of furloughs, accidents, and unexpected illness do not phase you. Life happens. Start with a six-month goal of saving half your paycheck. Over the next six months, save 5 percent of your gross income. You'll be amazed to discover you don't miss it at all.

Once you accomplish these steps of tidying up your finances, establish your budget.

Budgeting sources are highlighted in Pillar III: Be Disciplined, Reflection: Budget.

Questions to Answer:

⊃ Why is important to declutter our finances?
⊃ What five steps will you take to start the tidying up process?

Reflection: Arcade Fire's "Everything Now"

Instant gratification is the way of our day. We want what we want, and we want it now. But that's not the way God describes our journey with Him.

Good planning and hard work lead to prosperity, but hasty shortcuts lead to poverty.

Proverbs 21:5 (NLT)

"Good planning and hard work" are the opposite of instant gratification. The microwave way of thinking and functioning will take away our resources. Those who demand "everything now" in an instant will become poor. Be thoughtful, diligent and plan ahead, then God will bless our work and efforts with true gratification.

Many presume instant results are sustainable and indicate the right direction. Arcade Fire's song "Everything Now" describes our culture's skewed priorities based on short-term results and flexible values.

When I was in college, I remember trying to take advantage of every opportunity that came my way. I studied abroad in Paris, France; worked an internship; pledged a sorority; academically soared, and found my husband. Whew! Then I graduated and needed to 'marinate' because of the shift in my life. As a wife and then a new mom, life slowed down. Everything was not now.

Careful preparation and wise planning, along with diligence, result in long term success.

William H. Whyte wrote in the 1950s, "Remember, luck is what happens when preparation meets opportunity."

Careful preparation and wise planning, along with diligence, result in long term success.

Questions to Answer:

⊃ Have you ever had the "everything "now" attitude?

⊃ What was the result?

⊃ What could have been done differently to produce more sustainable and desirable outcomes?

⊃ Share an example of a time when you did prepare, plan, and maximize your opportunity.

Reflection: Be Intentional

My husband and I went to dinner with our eldest child and spouse. The couple said their focus this year was to be intentional.

We discussed how that looks in everyday life. We must vigorously pursue without becoming distracted, frustrated, or sidetracked by life's occurrences. And there are good, concrete steps we can take:

First, you must be clear about your goal. Pray and confirm the direction you are moving to.

Second, reorganize your life around that purpose.

Third, identify obstacles and plan how to overcome and react to them.

Fourth, prioritize your schedule such that you may achieve momentum toward fulfilling it.

Fifth, seek and ask for help. "Plans fail for lack of counsel, but with many advisers they succeed" Proverbs 15:22 (NIV).

Six, solicit an accountability partner.

Seven, be flexible and open.

Eight, persevere.

Nine, count the costs.

Ten, take the leap. #seize the moment.

Fear not, for I am with you.

Isaiah 41:10 (NKJV)

Questions to Answer:

- ⊃ How can you be more intentional?
- ⊃ What plan will you establish to make your dreams a reality?
- ⊃ List three steps you will take this year in being more intentional.

Reflection: Just Try it for 30 Days

A Child Shall Lead

When our son was a freshman in high school, he played basketball on one of our nation's leading high school teams. After the Saturday night game, many of the boys would come and spend the night. We had a wonderful time getting to know our son's teammates.

If everyone was ready before 9:00 a.m. Sunday, we stopped by McDonald's, then went to church. As time progressed, the boys started coming over every Saturday night, and their girlfriends and families would join them at the service.

The boys often questioned our son about why he had money all the time. Among other things, he told them about his habit of tithing.

So, he gave away more, then had more? It didn't make sense to the boys, just as it doesn't to the rest of the world. It simply works because God honors our obedience. Our son challenged his teammates to tithe for 30 days.

It's been ten-plus years since, and these young men are powerful believers and generous in their giving to God.

Questions to Answer:

⊃ Elaborate on what you are doing to encourage generosity and discipleship in your youth.

⊃ Have you tried giving generously to a house of worship?

⊃ What are you willing to try for 30 days?

Reflection: Curse of the Black Cat

I read on the website Petside.com about the famous superstition, "don't let a black cat cross your path." Out of the countless baseless superstitions known to our culture, this is one of the most popular and pervasive. Nearly everybody has heard it.

Supposedly, the person whose path the cat crossed is going to have bad luck.

The fear of black cats seems to trace back to the time shortly after the pilgrims arrived at Plymouth Rock. These settlers were actually devout Christians. They were highly suspicious of anything symbolic of evil or seemingly connected to the devil. In British and Western European traditions, black cats were seen as companion animals or "familiars" to witches.

In fact, sometimes people could be severely punished—even executed—simply for possessing a black cat.

As more Christians came to America, the myths took on even more power. Puritans sometimes believed witches transformed into the black cats to escape detection. Today, the superstition lives on, and some animal shelters won't offer a black cat for adoption. There's too much chance of animal abuse.

One day, I walked toward my car in snow and ice, and I saw one of these felines. I don't believe in silly superstitions, however, so I only smiled and kept walking. But when the cat crossed the street and headed my way . . . I found myself hurrying, and I almost slipped on a path of ice.

I felt silly—endangering myself because of a meaningless legend. Then I had a strong thought: How many of us change our behavior because of things we know are false—while refusing to change for the truth of God's Word?

How many of us change our behavior because of things we know are false

Malachi 3 says we are cursed with a curse because we withhold tithes and offerings. Yet the promise of blessings is there if we do as God instructs.

Questions to Answer:

⊃ Describe a situation when you adjusted your behavior on behalf of a lie.

⊃ When have you believed God or not believed Him?

⊃ Discuss your experiences.

⊃ What lessons did you learn?

Reflection: Intentional Giving

Giving doesn't come naturally to people because of our fallen human condition. Even though nothing is more satisfying, we won't do it in most cases unless we're proactive—intentional—about doing it. There's a clear-cut process to help encourage intentional giving in your family's life.

1. Pray. Bring all to the altar to pray about giving intentionally.
2. Plan and set your priorities.
3. Budget. Write down expenditure versus income.
4. Act with faith. Commit to a consistently increasing amount and share your testimony with others. Focus on the sacrifice and change in lifestyle, not the money. People want to know how it changes you positively, not how hard it was for you to do.

Questions to Answer:

⊃ How will you implement these steps to accelerate your giving?

⊃ What can you change in your lifestyle to allow you to give more intentionally?

⊃ Write down what you will do differently. Examples include:

✓ Downsizing and selling excess online; using buy/sell apps; through consignment.

✓ Minimizing certain activities. For example, instead of two manicures/haircuts a month, limit it to one. Prepare meals at home instead of eating out.

Reflection: Turn On

This slang phrase turn on caught my attention. What turns you on? Why?

Most of us are intentional about celebrating something grand such as:

- ⊃ a career move
- ⊃ a new life
- ⊃ a relationship
- ⊃ losing weight
- ⊃ financial win
- ⊃ victory over a challenge

But what about spiritual turn-ons? What are the intangible, heart-felt parts of life that make you glow all over? How about . . .

- ⊃ salvation
- ⊃ generosity
- ⊃ joining a church
- ⊃ changing a friend's life for the better
- ⊃ peace
- ⊃ joy
- ⊃ love

Turn On 4 Christ

As you pursue financial wellness, turn on for each milestone you make. Celebrate every single positive step you take. If you want to make an unworthy purchase and you succeed in walking away from it—feel good about that! Tell your friends and family. Mark your victory.

Question to Answer:

⊃ Talk about a turn-on moment in your life.

Reflection: Sit Down and Enjoy the Meal Before You Go for More

One night, I dreamed my church was in the midst of a celebration.

I was sitting near one of the mothers of the church. I offered to fix her plate since the food was at different stations and she is elderly. I started to do that, and I walked away to talk to someone and left the plate. When I turned around, someone had taken it.

So I started over. I went to other food stations and loaded a plate for her and one for me. Then I saw a station with luscious fruit. I put the plates down and went over to put some fruit on smaller plates. On my way back, I kept my eye on our full plates. As I approached our plates, a server grabbed the plates and threw them in the trash!

My heart sank, not only because of the time I spent meticulously preparing and selecting foods but also because of my absolute dislike of waste.

I learned my lesson. This time, I grabbed the salad and fruit, gave it to the church elder, then went back and fixed her plate. After all that was done, I took care of myself.

My elder looked at me, starved, as if to say "What happened?" Everyone else had finished eating. I apologized and finally sat down and enjoyed my meal.

Take the time to appreciate what you have on your "plate" before heaping on extra servings.

Questions to Answer:

- Describe a time when putting too much on your plate made you unproductive.
- Take a good, hard look at what you have ahead. Determine the best way to handle all your responsibilities.

Reflection: FOCUS

An intelligent person aims at wise action,
but a fool starts off in many directions.

Proverbs 17:24 (GNT)

Now more than ever before, we're pulled in different directions—so much to occupy our minds and our lives.

Social media exacerbates our attempts to rest and have mindfulness. Focus is an asset and rarely occurs. Yet, in order to propel to new levels of excellence and impact, we must set goals and prioritize our schedule and attention.

The pings of our phones and devices take precedence over almost everything else. Still, it's part of our lives. Rid yourself of the pings and pop up notifications. Remove social media from your front page. Schedule a limited set time to interact socially through social media and digitally. Go back to old fashioned note writing and phone calls, even consider visiting.

To achieve goals, we must set aside noise and separate ourselves. Mediation and prayer allow us to hear and see things important. Clearing our mind allows a creative flow that will bring us higher in our capacity to function and achieve.

Every morning, I spend quiet prayer time listening for God's direction. This gives me the reassurance that my path is blessed and aligned with what God would have me to do and/or accomplish. Also, I experience peace in unexpected or difficult situations.

Wise action takes focus. Propelling to new levels of excellence and impact, we must focus on achieving goals and reaching higher than we can envision.

Questions to Answer:

⊃ What are you focused on?

⊃ What have you done about the distractions of social media, text, and your smartphone?

Guidepost Scriptures for Further Reading on Being Disciplined

⊃ Luke 22:31-32
⊃ Psalms 1:3
⊃ Philippians 3:13-14
⊃ Hebrews 12:1

Pillar 11: Be a Masterpiece

For we are God's masterpiece. He has created us anew in Christ Jesus, so we can do the good things He planned for us long ago.

Ephesians 2:10 (NLT)

A masterpiece is an artist's greatest achievement—a work of consummate skill.

When we view a masterpiece, we feel deep admiration; perhaps even a sense of awe. Here is high art, supreme craftsmanship, something that will last.

The verse above, Ephesians 2:10, tells us that God, the artist of all creation, considers us his masterpiece. Have you taken that in? You are a work of awesome art and creativity. In the universe, you are as good as it gets! God says so.

All you have to do is to live that way.

In this Pillar, you will think about:

⊃ How you answer your why.
⊃ The impact you want to have in this world.
⊃ Whether you have experienced tragedy and how you're healing.

- What brings you peace and confidence.
- How your uniqueness can be an asset.
- How well you resist the desire to pursue riches.
- How you will leave a legacy.
- The torch you carry from those who went ahead of you.

DEFINE YOUR MISSION

Reflection: Discover Your Essence

When we look at a masterpiece, we see something perfectly suited to be itself. It's the prize specimen of its type, whether it's a painting, a fantastic song—or you.

God bought us here to be unique pieces in his master plan.

My mother certainly exhibited how to be a masterpiece, every day and every way. Recently, she left this world, and we know that everything and everyone she touched is better because of her. My sister cousin, Valerie Brown Traore, spoke about Mom's legacy, and I thought I would share her wisdom with you.

The Essence of Beulah

On behalf of the family, we thank you for being with us today as we celebrate the homecoming of a great woman of faith, love, and charity. Your presence here affirms for us how widely she was loved and admired.

Emeril Lagasse has a seasoning called the essence, with its blend of the right type of spices, herbs and other stuff to bring out the flavor of a dish. Well, we the family, have our blend that has been fermented and shelf-stable for almost 88 years, and we call it the Essence of Beulah. She's been the spice that has flavored our family in so many profound and lasting ways, whether that was as the devoted daughter, the bride of her Max, mom to her girls and sons-in-law, granny, sister, auntie, or cousin—she's our essence.

So, what is the Essence of Beulah? Well, let me break down some of the ingredients.

Turmeric is used to control inflammation. In any family or relationship, there will be misunderstandings. And you wish you had a fork to eat back some of the words that got exchanged. But if you had the good sense to go to Aunt Bea ahead of time, you'd learn such things as calm down, pray first, remember your vows, remember you wanted children, etc.

But most importantly, she showed through example that to forgive is to show love, and that love is a healing emotion. That's the anti-inflammatory effect she had on you.

The other ingredient in the essence of Beulah is the herb sage. Sage increases brain function and memory. For us, nobody on the planet was smarter than Aunt Bea. She was the go-to for everything related to education, the written or spoken word. She had an incredible gift of taking your unfiltered and chaotic thoughts and putting them just the right way, then coaching you on how to deliver it in the most elegant oral prose.

My personal story is that I had a debilitating speech impediment: I stuttered. But Aunt Bea refused to let me use that as an excuse. She became my speech therapist. She signed me up for every speaking part there was in this church. Because she knew it was my confidence that needed to be fixed first, and then the speech problem would fix itself.

She firmly believed that anyone with a willingness and determination could learn. She instilled in all of us the importance of education because with education, you have options; and with options, you have freedom.

Yes, your brain function increased when you were with her. She is sage.

And finally, there is the ingredient cinnamon, that sweet spice. Cinnamon lowers blood sugar levels. Well, when your blood sugars levels are balanced, you feel better all over. And she could do that through a smile, a " Hi, Baby," a gentle talk, or through a serving of her famous macaroni and cheese and potato salad. Holidays at 3620 W. Forest Park were the highlight of our year, especially at Christmas. The house was filled with so much good food, love, and laughter with the fellowship of family and family-like friends.

One of the things you learned early growing up in Forest Park was not to get attached to your Christmas gift. Aunt Bea was famous for re-gifting. The perfume collection she just gave you could easily become the new gift for an unexpected guest.

And if it snowed that Christmas, the day after was like the after-party. Aunt Bea and Uncle Troy would open up the house, and we'd all gather again, eating the good leftovers, while the adults would be upstairs talking smack at the pinochle table—Uncle Troy being the biggest smack talker, but he was the best player, too.

You know, Maya Angelou said people might not always remember what you said, but they always remember how you made them feel. That's Aunt Bea; she just knew how to make you feel good. She was cinnamon—magnified!

> Maya Angelou said people might not always remember what you said, but they always remember how you made them feel.

Five minutes is surely not enough to tell you all the ingredients in the Essence of Beulah, but if you look at her family, Uncle Troy—her girls, the grands—you'll see that essence, and also in those of us whose lives have been improved because of her presence. We too know the Essence of Beulah.

Questions to Answer:

- ⊃ What legacy do you want to leave?
- ⊃ How will you elevate your behavior and actions to become more impactful?

Reflection: Flawed Leadership

In Mark 15, Pilate turns against what he believes is right and gives the crowd what they demand. He inspects Jesus, interviews him, and personally concludes he sees nothing wrong with this quiet man before him.

But the mob is loud and unruly. It yells, "Crucify!" And Pilate values peace and quiet more than justice, so he gives the loudest voices what they want.

Sometimes in life, we must do something uncommon, uncomfortable, and unpopular just because our inner self tells us what is right according to God.

Have you ever felt swayed by those around you toward doing what the "still, small voice" inside you counseled you to avoid? What decides your actions: conscience or the crowd?

Lesson: Discern and pray for clarity and don't let the loud voices and noises take you off course.

Questions to Answer:

⊃ Write about an instance when you listened to others despite your inner longings to go a different route.

⊃ How will you prepare for a leadership role and discern the 'right' direction?

⊃ List five steps you will take and when you will implement each.

Reflection: Your Organic Self

I was walking the streets of New York City with the founder of an international nonprofit. He commented on my "natural" hair. He said he really liked my "twists updo" (hair up with natural texture) the most. He remembered the original video conference call with me and seeing my curly twists. He said he really liked the fact that I was my organic self.

My hair was hip, according to this leader—current; in other words, I was simply being myself.

He explained that many female Jewish relatives of his would straighten their hair or even put chemicals in it. He didn't understand why, since their hair was naturally curly and full.

People want you to be your organic self because that's the version of you that God designed for this world.

Oh yes, you shaped me first inside, then out; you formed me in my mother's womb. I thank you, High God--you're breathtaking! Body and soul, I am marvelously made! I worship in adoration--what a creation! You know me inside and out, you know every bone in my body; You know exactly how I was made, bit by bit, how I was sculpted from nothing into something. Like an open book, you watched me grow from conception to birth; all the stages of my life were spread out before you, the days of my life all prepared before I'd even lived one day.

Psalm 139:13

My nonprofit colleague was referring to outward appearances, of course. What really counts is the inner person. As Jesus put it, God looks upon the heart. He shaped and formed us for his special purposes, inside and out, and life is all about being the best version of the creature he made us to be.

Questions to Answer:

◌ What is unique about you that you may try to change or cover up?

◌ How can your uniqueness be an asset?

Reflection: Turn Around

Yesterday, a doe (a female deer) jumped our fence and was "stuck" in the backyard. Our fence is six feet high, and she couldn't find her way out. The doe was obsessed with the back portion of the yard fence because she knew her mom and siblings were there.

The doe kept focusing on the back fence. Meanwhile, the gate to the fence was wide open and waiting, but she only had eyes for what was right in front of her. Ultimately, she hurt her shoulder when she tried leaping over that fence and came up short.

Sometimes, our blessing is right behind or beside us. We just need to look around and see the opening! Our problem is only looking in the most obvious direction.

We just need to look around and see the opening!

Think outside your box and look around. The opening may be just out of eyesight but wide open and waiting.

Question to Answer:

➲ Describe a situation when you kept looking for answers in the wrong direction.

Reflection: Being First

Master something! Find out what it is you do really well and pour yourself into achieving the highest grade of excellence at it.

Malcolm Gladwell, in his book *Outliers*, discusses our contemporary gurus who mastered their crafts and were tops in their fields. They were trailblazers who not only set the pace—they also blazed a new path that caught fire.

Not everyone will be a Bill Gates or an Oprah Winfrey. Everyone would like to be the kind of athlete LeBron James is, or the kind of musician Aretha Franklin was. Still, in our own sphere of influence, we may blaze a path and soar.

Strive to be the pacesetter!

He has created us anew in Christ Jesus,
so we can do the good things he planned for us long ago.

Ephesians 2:10 (NLT)

Questions to Answer:

⊃ Where can you be a master?

⊃ What are you uniquely made to do?

⊃ Post three areas you believe you may master.

Reflection: The "Flourishing" Business Model

We hear a lot about *flourishing* these days. "May you flourish and be at peace." To flourish is to thrive, to be strong and well. A key Scripture for this idea is:

The righteous will flourish like a palm tree,
they will grow like a cedar of Lebanon.

Psalm 92:12

May the Lord cause you to flourish,
both you and your children.

Psalm 115:14 (NIV)

The steps to flourishing are:

1. Have a Vision.

Make sure your vision is clear and includes the four 'I's:

- ⊃ *Information*: Comprehensive and concise description of the vision, what you hope to achieve, and the path to moving from where you are to your ultimate destination.
- ⊃ *Impact*: Using stories about one person or family that was impacted. Walk readers through the situation so that they may grasp the severity of the story. Tie the vision directly to the situation and show in real terms the positive result.
- ⊃ *Inspiration*: Helping your readers visualize the story. Integrating emotional elements that will ignite their desire to support the vision. Creating a sense of urgency.
- ⊃ *Investment*: Asking! Asking and asking again for a fiscal investment or involvement. Making it easy to respond and/or ask questions.

2. Create a Plan.

Build a framework for how you may achieve your vision. Make sure it is well-resourced and has fiscal stability. Seek wise advice from experts. Use a collaborative project management tool like Teamwork (www.teamwork.com) that manages tasks, milestones, messaging, files, and your calendar. This will keep you on track and help you to adjust your path as appropriate. Also, process your map to lay out your plan and its components visually.

3. Execute with Excellence.

Quality is a priority—continuing in your striving to accomplishing much. Above all else, remember relationships first, then money, tasks, and things. Do not compromise values nor take shortcuts.

4. Remove Obstacles.

Stay the course and plan for bumps. Proper forethought and preparation are key to a smooth path. Give yourself space for unanticipated roadblocks. Recover quickly and forge ahead.

Our business is to resource God's vision through his people and God's flow, setting the captives free from bondage.

Our Flourish Business Model includes:

- ⊃ Financial freedom for God's people and his nonprofits.
- ⊃ Lifestyle stewardship.
- ⊃ Debt elimination.
- ⊃ Resourcing God's kingdom here on earth.

Question to Answer:

 ⊃ What five steps will you implement to flourish and make your vision a reality?

Reflection: Doing Our Assignment

Recently, I heard someone speaking about Martin Luther King and his "I Have a Dream" speech during the Poor People's March on Washington on August 28, 1963. What a prophetic voice. One-quarter of a million people were there to hear it, gathered together on the steps of the Lincoln Memorial.

As Dr. King started his speech, Mahalia Jackson turned toward him and said, "Tell them about the Dream, Martin, Tell them about the Dream."

Martin pushed his prepared speech aside and let the Holy Spirit take over. He spoke from the heart, and God filled that heart with his power and with the kind of words people never forget—the kind of words that shape the course of history.

Dr. King delivered America's prophecy through his "I have a Dream" speech. But this kind of thing isn't limited to the heroes of history. God wants to speak through all of us. He wants to use us to change this world for the better.

Are you ready to put aside your prepared program for the day and act precisely according to his will for you?

Questions to Answer:

⊃ Have you ever prepared to do something and, after someone or something redirected you, it was better than you imagined?

⊃ Discuss what happened.

⊃ What gave you the assurance to move forward?

Reflection: Emotional Quotient (EQ)

Nearly everyone has heard of IQ (intelligence quotient). Did you know we can, in a sense, quantify the work of the heart just as well as the work of the mind?

Emotional Quotient (EQ)is the level of a person's emotional intelligence, often represented by a score on a standardized test. Travis Bradberry and Jean Greaves are responsible for this fascinating way of understanding how we act and react.

EQ is how well we recognize and understand our own emotions and those of others; and how we differentiate our assortment of feelings. We use this emotional information in an instinctive way, without even realizing it, to guide us through life. A four-year-old child will react to disappointment in a different way than a forty-year-old adult. How high is your EQ? What happens? How do we understand it? How do we react?

EQ is how well we recognize and understand our own emotions and those of others

When I first joined Boys & Girls Clubs of America (BGCA) as Vice President, it was important to be mentored by someone that understood the culture and had successfully navigated the landscape. Frank Sanchez, a younger Hispanic single father, who had grown up in the clubs was selected to mentor me. He rose to executive leadership status because of his high EQ (emotional quotient) & leadership skills.

Still, I had very little in common with Frank as a married mother and pastor's wife, who did not know what EQ was, much less how to use it to lead my region. He was a master at navigating relationships and had a high EQ. Soon after joining BGCA, there was a national employee recognition event. The purpose was to celebrate the leadership and accomplishments of stellar employees. Frank escorted me there and placed me next to another leader who was well-known and respected. After introducing us, Frank went to sit at another table. I was overwhelmed by the passion of the employees and sat there trying to absorb it all. The time came when the President of BGCA gave the 'epitome of leadership award.' The leader next to me was the recipient of this award. He was so surprised and blushed when hundreds of employees stood and applauded for him. Frank had the wisdom to sit me next to him.

Frank showed me how to build effective teams internal & external to BGCA by valuing those who think differently and using their most stellar competencies to propel team effectiveness and productivity. By the end of the year, my region led the country in establishing new corporate partnerships and was well on its way to significantly exceeding fiscal goals. My career at BGCA took off because of the example of leaders like Frank.

EQ has four components:

- Self-awareness
- Self-management
- Relationship management
- Social awareness

I look at EQ as the bridge between reality and perception.

Questions to Answer:

- Describe a scenario when you displayed a "low" EQ.
- What exactly happened? What should have happened?
- How can you build your EQ?

Reflection: Shoe on the Right Foot

On some occasion, when you were getting dressed while still half-asleep, did you ever put the left shoe on the right foot?

It feels awkward. We can't imagine taking a single step until we've gotten the correct feet into the correct shoes!

Imagine living an entire life in which you're trying to fit a left shoe on a right foot, pushing a square peg in a round hole, or forcing a jigsaw puzzle piece into the slot where it doesn't belong. A mismatched life creates stress, anxiety, and unhappiness all around.

It could be the wrong career, an unhappy marriage or an inappropriate lifestyle.

Is there a portion of your experience that simply feels out of joint and wrong?

Questions to Answer:

➲ What one part of your life would you "refit" right now if you had the opportunity?

➲ What practical steps can you take to do something about it?

Reflection: The Impact of Labels

Today, I was at the nail salon, receiving a manicure from my favorite technician, Sophia.

Sophia grew up in Vietnam. She and her brother were close until they went to middle school at the age of nine. They all had to take a test, a difficult test that measured their intelligence. The results of the test determined their placement for the rest of their academic career.

There were three tracks: Advanced Placement (AP) for smart kids; average placement for students who scored okay but not great; and lastly, the school for the "slower" kids who didn't do well on the test.

So, if you're not a good test taker, sometimes there's no chance of receiving an academically challenging curriculum, and college is out.

Sophia is a vivacious reader and speaker. However, she could not score well on the test. Her oldest sister made it into the AP school; Sophia did average. Her brother only scored well enough to go to the lowest school. This caused a separation in the family.

Sophia observed that people were labeled according to their school. You could not go beyond your designated school even if you did well. There was a stigma placed on you. She remembers her cousin was in the smart kids' school, and that made a huge difference in how that cousin was accepted.

Even though Sophia and her cousin were the same age, the family respected her cousin more and cheered her on. Sophia had very good social skills; still, those did not surpass the cultural focus on intelligence and success in school.

I saw the sadness in Sophia's eyes as she reflected on the stigma of being labeled "less than."

I explained to her that everyone has a unique gift and is brilliant at something. Sophia explained that the school system has changed. Still, her culture puts such a strong emphasis on academic success, and it's all some can see.

everyone has a unique gift and is brilliant at something

Sophia understands now that she is gifted in her own way. Yet the sting of rejection and limited opportunity still exists. Sophia has learned not to evaluate herself on how others see her.

Questions to Answer:

⊃ Have you put emphasis on one talent—say, "book smarts"—at the expense of not recognizing another?

⊃ Have you been the victim or even the beneficiary of the "smart" kid label?

⊃ What childhood labels haunt you today?

LIVE YOUR MISSION

Reflection: Plot the Path to Success

To define and plot your path, you must first recognize where you are.

Many mornings, I watch the sunrise. Seeing God's natural alarm clock, the dawning of a new day— "new mercies do I see each morning."

> I watch the sunrise. Seeing God's natural alarm clock

Hearing the birds chirp awakens me with hope for the new day. This morning, God placed on my heart this question: "*Where* are you?"

I didn't know in geographical terms which were east, west, north, or south. So, I plotted the path. Specifically, I placed my position on a map, defining each direction in terms of where I currently was positioned.

Then the revelation came. Sure, my husband and I know where our businesses are now. We know where we want our businesses to take us. Still, what we must plot out is how long we should go on in that direction before heading another way.

Know where you are and how to move forward, step by step.

Questions to Answer:

- Define where you are fiscally.
- Determine where you want to be and when.
- Plot out seven milestones with time parameters to achieve your destiny.

Reflection: Independence Day

God has set me free to pursue and become prosperous in my purpose in life. *I am not for sale.*

My pastor wrote a compelling reference letter that touched me deeply. Another respected colleague looked deep into my heart and eyes and said, "You are anointed and called to do this work. You will soar beyond anyone's expectations. Your ministry is to help churches and others realize God's vision for their territory. You will impact many."

I felt such reassurance!

I'm free to be what God wants me to be; free from the expectations of others; free from the pull of poor choices in life. I know where I am, where I'm going, and I know the Spirit of God provides the wind in my sails.

Questions to Answer:

⊃ Are you free to pursue your purpose in life?

⊃ Has anyone spoken into your life when you needed it most?

⊃ Have you sincerely encouraged anyone today?

Reflection: Rich and Famous

As I speak with many today, I notice that most of them desire to be rich; to have access and live a life like the Kardashians, JayZ and Beyoncé, or even their richest friend. With the glitz and glamour of social media, advertising, and biased reporting, it's difficult to distinguish fact from fiction when it comes to "the good life." Is it really all it's cracked up to be?

First, we don't know about the lives of these celebrities. Do they have peace, love, and fulfillment?

Second, *all* of us are designed for a purpose, and our focus should be on fulfilling what we are designed to do— nothing more, nothing less. Contentment comes not in how many toys we accumulate, but in how well we fulfill our God-given purpose.

> *our focus should be on fulfilling what we are designed to do*

Third, ultimately, we control nothing. At most, we can do what God instructs us to do.

We do know this: he promises he will reward the diligent.

So, don't believe the hype! Know you are a masterpiece, uniquely designed by God to accomplish much. *Period.* And if you accomplish the "much" he has set out, you'll be more successful than any celebrity, any billionaire, any ruler.

Questions to Answer:

➲ How do you resist the desire to pursue riches?

➲ Write about a scenario where you made a poor decision based on the pursuit of riches.

Reflection: 3-D Choices

What should I do?

When you are at a crossroads, not knowing how to proceed, take a 3-D view: three-dimensional.

If you watch an ordinary movie, it's "flat." It has length and width, two dimensions. But put on your 3-D glasses, and wow! Now that picture seems to be coming out of the screen. It has a third dimension: depth.

When confronted with a difficult decision, taking a 3-D view allows us to see a decision, not only from an immediate perspective but also a broader perspective. You see it *in-depth.*

Look at short-term benefits, long-range plans, and impact assessment.

Go back to what you are designed to accomplish.

Consider:

ᕱ Quality of Life
ᕱ Fulfilling my Life Purpose
ᕱ Advancing my goal to help others move up the ladder from debt to becoming:

1. Financially Stable, then …
2. Financially Free, then …
3. Financially Secure!

Questions to Answer:

ᕱ What process do you undertake to make decisions and to chart your path?

ᕱ How will you become financially secure?

Reflection: Remain Humble Despite Elevation

As my gifts manifest, as I feel satisfied with my work, as I'm tempted toward self-importance—I must remember I'm only dirt!

Yes, I'm a creature God molded out of the dust of the earth. Without him, I'm nothing. Any exaltation is his doing, not mine. He rescued me from the snare of my enemy. By his might *only* am I able to go forth boldly in confidence and love.

There are periods in my life where I soar. My gifts become manifest and have significant results and impact. Despite obstacles, I push forward. I land in places I don't deserve nor could have dreamt possible.

After completing high school in three years instead of four, I attended the first degree-granting historically black college, Lincoln University in Pennsylvania, with a full scholarship. Brown University in Rhode Island and the University of Maryland College Park had accepted me; still Lincoln was my destiny.

Immediately, I was a lioness! I knew I was at home. At 17 years old, I met the love of my life, and we have been together ever since. Highlights of being a student at Lincoln included joining Alpha Kappa Alpha Sorority, doing a semester of cooperative study in my field, dancing until the sun came up, and studying a semester in Paris, France.

During that time abroad, I came to know God personally and accepted Jesus as my Lord and Savior. Graduating from Lincoln as both class president and valedictorian was so exhilarating! Shortly after graduation, my college sweetheart and I married. We had a huge wedding, sponsored by the world's best parents; everyone we loved came together to celebrate our union.

This was a period of elevation in my life. Even though there were rough times, they only served to strengthen me and my faith.

Still, I recalled all those who helped me and particularly God who made me. I remembered that many did not have my fortune. As I matured, I learned gratitude and the importance of expressing it to others. Just as important is having empathy and compassion for all those who suffer and are not as fortunate.

Seasons come and go in our lives, yet God never sleeps, never takes a day off, never stops blessing us.

Questions to Answer:

⊃ Describe a time you have soared.

⊃ How can you regain that momentum?

⊃ Are you sensitive to others who may not be as fortunate?

Reflection: New Beginnings

Begin anew! How important is it to retain a sense of being a new creation and experiencing God's tender mercies every day, when they're new? It makes every day on the calendar an adventure.

Tomorrow, when I return to work, I know it's just one day. Still, it's a new beginning.

I have butterflies, yet I'm not panicking.

The word for this 6 a.m. prayer call was optimism. I'll walk in God's authority, prepared for what he has for me. He has sent his ministering angels before me. I believe. My attitude is positive. I claim the power behind this verse: "Be anxious for nothing" (Philippians 4:6, NIV).

What I've given you above is the mental framework I strive to maintain during smooth sailing and troubled waters alike. I see every day as a new opportunity, even if it seems like a new obstacle.

I see every day as a new opportunity, even if it seems like a new obstacle.

In times of difficulty and uncertainty, stay calm. Meditate on good things, keep your peace, and be grateful for security. Focus on your reason for being and do not be distracted. Confidently move forward in your purpose.

Question to Answer:

⊃ What brings you peace and confidence? Use that thought in an hour of uncertainty.

Reflection: All that God Wants is Our Best

Believe that God is there for you. Believe he will honor your obedience from day to day, from moment to moment; that doing the right thing, walking the straight path leads to the right destination because he will never fail you.

"He is a rewarder of those who diligently seek Him" (Hebrews 11:6, NKJV). We are "created in Christ Jesus to do good works, which God prepared in advance for us to do" (Ephesians 2:10, NIV).

During the time of transition from my former employer, my dream shifted—not because of my will, but my understanding of God's will.

"And we know that in all things God works for the good of those who love him, who have been called according to his purpose" (Romans 8:28 NIV).

As Proverbs 16:3 tells us, let's commit our work to the Lord, knowing our plans will succeed.

Questions to Answer:

⊃ Describe a time in your life where you experienced disappointment and it turned out better for you in the end.

Reflection: Life on Pause

When you don't see progress in your life, you may be at the point where your life is on pause. What do you do?

- Seek healing and inner peace.
- Be excellent where you are.
- Do what you always wanted to do but never had the time.
- Plan for success.
- Appreciate what you do have.
- Trust God.
- Be prepared to pivot.

Sometimes, life is paused because of tragedy, significant loss (like that of a spouse or child), illness, unemployment, or broken dreams. Still, we have to push through.

My oldest sister experienced unbelievable loss in a two-year period. She lost her dream job partly because she spent so much time helping to care for our ailing parents. Before she could recover and seek other employment, her college sweetheart and husband unexpectedly took his last breath.

She decided not to return to the house they'd shared for over thirty years. Their house lost significant value and needed many repairs. Before she could stand on her own again, her baby, the youngest son of two, was killed suddenly in a car accident.

Her son and his fiancé were about to send out announcements of their wedding. Those wedding "save the date" cards became my nephew's memorial announcement cards. Devastated yet not destroyed, my sister trusted God and pushed through.

My sister's example taught me so much about not looking at bare circumstances, yet seeking God's purpose and trusting Him. She preached a sermon called "Between a Rock and a Hard Place." That certainly describes where she was, yet she realized her feet were on the Rock, the solid foundation of Christ.

"Between a Rock and a Hard Place."

By the way, my sister is flying high now. She returned to school to pursue her Masters. She also was appointed as a Pastor of a small church. She now resides in her baby son's former home. Best of all, my sister has become a supreme comforter to those who experience significant loss and devastation.

She is one of my 'she-roes.'

Questions to Answer:

⊃ Discuss a time your life was on pause.

⊃ What three lessons are you able to learn from survivors?

⊃ Have you experienced tragedy, and how are you healing?

Reflection: Samson's Hair Cut

When I was with one of my former employers, I felt as if Delilah cut my hair—snipping away my strength and gift. I was sapped of the energy God wanted me to have.

Now, being at my new place of employment, God has caused my hair (gifts) to grow thicker, longer and stronger. I feel healthy. My gift never left me and is now manifested much stronger.

Was I at a place that strangled my being? That smothered my capability? That took away my strength? Have you ever been in such a situation?

Sometimes, we don't shine because our environment is toxic and unhealthy.

On the other hand, we can't always blame our surroundings. The problem may lie with our own thinking and thoughts or beliefs that limit our progress.

What about you?

> *Sometimes, we don't shine because our environment is toxic and unhealthy.*

Questions to Answer:

⊃ Are you in a healthy environment that is causing you to flourish?

⊃ How may you change your thoughts to ensure that you soar?

Reflection: Stay in Your Lane; Empower the Right Ones

Scenario: I crafted a letter for the church to send about financial commitments to our campaign. Even though I asked that the letter be proofed, I missed several key elements—however, that was not the mistake.

I handed the baton to the wrong runner.

The draft should have gone to the director of that team, to the leader. She would have caught and added the details and then authorized the letter to be sent. If I'd empowered the director, the RSVP and time information would have been included. Instead, I wrote my article and handed it into someone who didn't have those details.

Live and learn!

Questions to Answer:

⊃ Have you ever stepped beyond your boundaries?

⊃ What was the result?

Reflection: You Are So Beautiful to Me

I spent the night with Mom and Dad. I couldn't sleep, not because of any noise in the house, but because my mind couldn't stop racing.

When I arose and dressed (halfway), I went to help Dad dress. He said, "You are a pretty girl." My parents love showering compliments on their children.

I said, "Thanks, Dad. Still, it's too early for me to look my best."

He replied, "That's the point! When you first wake up, that's when I can tell if you're pretty or not."

Mom said, "She sure is pretty, and she keeps her weight off."

Dad: "Carla you are so beautiful, I could cry."

Mom: "Now no one is *that* pretty."

We all laughed. I said, "Well I came from you two—so thanks!"

Question to Answer:

⊃ Take the time to spend time with those who encourage and lift you up.

Reflection: Bring God's Light Forward

I think often of my nephew Andrew. We didn't have him among us in this world nearly long enough. Yet in the time he was given, all too short as it was, he managed to shine God's light in a variety of ways.

Let his full, short life shine some of that light on us. As Andrew comes to mind, what I think about most are:

⊃ His full life
⊃ His wit
⊃ His charisma
⊃ His intelligence
⊃ His overcoming, zealous spirit.

Tears fill my eyes and my heart breaks, given his early departure. I'm moved to pray for:

⊃ His fiancé
⊃ His mother
⊃ His brother
⊃ His aunts
⊃ His grandfather
⊃ His frat brothers
⊃ All of us that knew and loved him

Still . . .

The following wise words from my departed nephew Andrew T. Brown, including his favorite quotations, still resonate and guide us:

⊃ "My goal in life is to help people be the best that they can be. I try to live by a few simple, yet powerful principles discovered by those wiser than I am."

⊃ "I don't care who gets the credit. I just want to win."

"My goal in life is to help people be the best that they can be.

⊃ "If you don't have time to do it right, will you have time to do it over?" –John Wooden

⊃ "Be a Blessing to Someone." –my Mom, Rev. Angela Maxwell Brown

⊃ "And now these three remain: faith, hope, and love. But the greatest of these is love" (1 Corinthians 13:13, NIV).

We are all blessed with various gifts and talents. But I truly believe we're called to love and support our fellow man. I believe the *why* is far more important than the *what* in terms of living a purpose-driven life. I don't know exactly where life will take me, but I do know that, when it's all said and done, I want to hear "Well done my Good and Faithful Servant.

Well Done Andrew! He wasn't perfect, but he left the imprint of himself everywhere and with everyone. I'll carry Andrew's torch forever as a reminder to bring God's light forward.

Questions to Answer:

⊃ How will you leave a legacy?

⊃ What torch are you carrying from others who have gone on?

Reflection: Inside Out

Oh yes, you shaped me first inside, then out; you formed me in my mother's womb. I thank you, High God—you're breathtaking! Body and soul, I am marvelously made! I worship in adoration—what a creation! You know me inside and out, you know every bone in my body; You know exactly how I was made, bit by bit, how I was sculpted from nothing into something. Like an open book, you watched me grow from conception to birth; all the stages of my life were spread out before you. The days of my life all prepared before I'd even lived one day.

Psalm 139:13-14, The Message

Yesterday, I visited my cousin in the hospital; she is clinging to life. She's my eldest cousin, and my twin and I are among the youngest.

Her desire to live is unparalleled. My family has the gift of perseverance, and my cousin is the epitome of that perseverance.

her illness bought together family like nothing else could

We talked about how God has a purpose for us all. We discussed how her illness bought together family like nothing else could. Family members that have not spoken in years are now at her bedside together.

My cousin smiled as a tear rolled down her face. She saw God using her to heal relationships and bring His love.

Questions to Answer:

⊃ Describe how suffering could bring or has bought healing in your life?

⊃ What path are you on toward fulfilling your purpose?

Reflection: The Epitome of Leadership

Fortune magazine's cover story for April is the "World's Greatest Leaders." It highlights the difference 50 outstanding leaders are making. They include Theo Epstein, John McCain (deceased), Pope Francis, Jack Ma, Bono, and Ava DuVernay.

Each has left—and is still leaving—a lasting legacy that positively impacts the lives of many. Each leader generously gives of themselves and their resources.

King David is the epitome of leadership, especially as we see in 1 Chronicles 28-29. In this passage, David sees the need to build a vast, worthy tabernacle to honor God. He realizes he will not be the chosen one to build this great building, yet he has garnered the resources to help fund it. God throughout gives us instructions on how to possess the land, not only for ourselves but for future generations.

David, as king, stepped up and gave abundantly and sacrificially out of his personal resources to help build the tabernacle. David challenged the leaders to join him in this journey of generosity. The masses rejoiced seeing the leaders give. They responded in joy and faith.

David reiterated that God is in control of everything, and that riches and honor come from God alone.

Then the celebration came, as all had prayed and given sacrificially. This is my ministry—to ensure that all God's people experience generosity.

We all interpret leadership differently. One of the most impactful leaders in my life was Kurt Aschermann, former Senior Vice President of Resource Development and Marketing at Boys and Girls Clubs of America (BGCA). Kurt sought me out and recruited me to BGCA. He was my supervisor. As a retired baseball coach, he had a coaching way of supervising. Kurt will show you how to do something, challenge you to do it better, and leave you alone. Kurt is a guru in Cause Marketing and taught me much of what he knew. He encouraged me to lead the Individual Giving Team for BGCA. In addition to leading my region, I took on this challenge. He did not leave me, nor did he look over my shoulder. When I doubted myself, Kurt reassured me that I had it in me and to go for it. As I result, the Individual Giving Team that I led, propelled annual individual giving for BGCA from raising a few million toward exponential growth.

I desire that we all become our *world's greatest leaders*—in our own sphere of influence.

Questions to Answer:

⊃ Are you leading in generosity?

⊃ If not, what is holding you back?

⊃ What three characteristics do you most admire in those who led or are leading you?

Reflection: Ordinary People Do the Extraordinary

Called for such a time as this.

That famous phrase comes from the Old Testament story of Esther.

The Bible is filled with narratives of women who exemplify timely callings. We have Rachel, Esther, Leah, Rahab, and of course, Mary, the mother of Jesus. All are ordinary women in extraordinary times.

Esther's story encourages us to do extraordinary things. Esther was called for such a time as this. Her cousin, Mordecai, came and spoke with her and called her to act courageously for God and for the safety of her people. God prepared her throughout her life to go, and she approached the King.

She was blessed with beauty. The King, attracted to Esther, listened to her pleas for her people. God uses her to save the Jewish nation.

None of us know the day or the hour that God will call us to do courageous acts. Still, we have to be open to his calling and open to his people. We are all called to do extraordinary things, even if we're just everyday individuals. We serve an extraordinary God.

We look at powerful leaders such as Harriet Tubman, who had a disability. She led hundreds of slaves to their freedom through the Underground Railroad. She was smart. She was patient. Harriet Tubman had the power of understanding her obstacles as opportunities. She seized her chance, and she took advantage of it.

> *Harriet Tubman had the power of understanding her obstacles as opportunities*

Another leader, Richard Allen, founder of the African Methodist Episcopal Church, was extraordinary yet ordinary. Rev. Allen and his wife Sarah joined forces with slaves and helped them to find their dignity and a place to freely worship and pray.

What ordinary trait will God use for extraordinary purposes?

Questions to Answer:

⊃ What extraordinary act have you accomplished that positively impacts others?

⊃ What calculated risks are you willing to take to help others?

⊃ List five steps to move you from ordinary to extraordinary.

Guidepost Scriptures for further reading on discipline:

⊃ Ecclesiastes 3:1
⊃ Proverbs 29:18
⊃ Psalm 139

Pillar III: Be Diligent

We want each of you to show this same diligence to the very end, so that what you hope for may be fully realized.

Hebrews 6:11

Diligence is careful, persistent effort. It's simple stick-to-it-iveness; you might even say it's stubbornness applied to a good cause.

You can exercise for a day and maybe for a week. But can you exercise for a month? A year? You can watch your diet for a day, maybe for a week. But how much longer?

"I never have any good luck," says the defeatist. "Nothing ever works out for me." Benjamin Franklin, however, said that "diligence is the mother of good luck." Plain old persistence will eventually meet opportunity, and the result is dream fulfillment.

In the parts of life that really count, it's not so much what you can do, but how long you can keep doing it. In the verse from Hebrews quoted above, we find out the fruit of diligence: "What you hope for may be fully realized." What do you hope for?

Isn't the object of your dearest hope worth a little diligence?

In this Pillar, you will think about:

⊃ How much you value hard work.
⊃ How persevering will help you to accomplish your goal.
⊃ How to develop a plan to save more.

DEFINE YOUR MISSION

Reflection: In Light of All This

In light of all this, here's what I want you to do. While I'm locked up here, a prisoner for the Master, I want you to get out there and walk— better yet, run!—on the road God called you to travel. I don't want any of you sitting around on your hands. I don't want anyone strolling off, down some path that goes nowhere. And mark that you do this with humility and discipline—not in fits and starts, but steadily, pouring yourselves out for each other in acts of love, alert at noticing differences and quick at mending fences.

Ephesians 4:1

Eugene Peterson, who wrote *The Message* paraphrase of Scripture, continues the passage above by telling the following story.

Christ climbed the highest of all mountains, captured the enemy, and claimed the treasure. Then he handed it all out as gifts to his people. Those are the spiritual gifts we have in Christ. Every single one of us possesses these greatest of all gifts: some as apostles, some as prophets, some as evangelists, some as teachers. Some are skilled in servant work or simple hospitality. But when we use our gifts together, we fall into a perfect rhythm, and we become fully alive in Christ.

Are you familiar and comfortable with your spiritual gift? Finding it and using it is the secret to fulfillment in life. So:

⊃ Be diligent, persevere, and be resilient.
⊃ Stay in your lane. Do what you are meant to do and don't become distracted.
⊃ Be steady.
⊃ Be uniquely you—your gift makes you just that.

Questions to Answer:

⊃ Do you know the path that you are to lead?

⊃ Are you striving to be more excellent with your gift?

⊃ What changes are you going to make?

Reflection: Achieving

Benjamin Elijah Mays said: "The tragedy of life doesn't lie in not reaching your goal. The tragedy lies in having no goal to reach. It isn't a calamity to die with dreams unfulfilled, but it is a calamity not to dream . . . It is not a disgrace not to reach the stars, but it is a disgrace to have no stars to reach for."

Benjamin Elijah Mays said: "The tragedy of life doesn't lie in not reaching your goal. The tragedy lies in having no goal to reach.

Failure isn't a sin. Low aim or no aim, however, is a tragedy.

My twin sister tells this story about why she was the first one born. Both of us were in Mom's womb waiting to come out. As she tells it, my sister glimpsed the tiniest peek at the light, and she headed out.

I too saw the opening. Still, she observes, I had to make a list of all I would accomplish in my life. My twin noted that we skipped a grade in high school, then I went on to Lincoln University on a full scholarship, graduated valedictorian of my class, traveled internationally, married my college sweetheart, had two children, and completed a marathon. It took me about seven minutes to double-check my list, then I headed out, ready to embrace life.

Yes, admittedly, I was born to accomplish much. We all are. In fact, when I took Tom Rath's Strength Finder 2.0, my top strength is *achiever*. The saying has some truth: When the student is ready, the teacher will come. Preparing to succeed and positioning yourself for elevation certainly are essential.

Intuitively, if we seek and open our minds and spirit, God will send us the resources and people to help actualize our accomplishments. So, I encourage you to reach for the stars, dream big, and make a list of all you will accomplish in life.

Questions to Answer:

⊃ What dream is pressing you forward?

⊃ Have you made your checklist?

Reflection: The Accomplisher: Get it Done

When you have the gift of achieving, you expect others to have the same gift. You think everybody is supposed to be racing to get things done.

Not so fast; you don't know what God has for others. Their gifts may be entirely different. Remember, we are together one unified body, and each component has a role.

I woke up this morning, thinking about the small tasks that others were to execute on behalf of our team. Many are complete; still, others are not. My husband especially did not fulfill his tasks. Yet his business is booming.

God put on my mind that not all have the gift of achieving; it's simply my particular gift and the lens through which I tend to view the world. While reminding my husband of his responsibilities, he looks at me and reminds me of his own gifts—which *I* don't have!

Unity in diversity makes us beautiful in harmony.

Questions to Answer:

- ⊃ What is your gift?
- ⊃ Do you expect others to do what you do well?
- ⊃ How can you use your gift for the elevation of teams?
- ⊃ Are you recognizing that we all have a unique purpose?

FUND YOUR MISSION

Reflection: Treasure in the Trash

My husband owns an estate/online sale business. We find that many times, after the death of a loved one, or some time when someone desires to downsize, the home is full of these old treasures. The children do not want the items that are left. So they contact my husband's company, Caring Transitions, to liquidate the estate.

This business success is based on the idea that one man's trash is another's treasure. Heirlooms left behind offer treasure-hunters the opportunity to acquire expensive items for little cost. Because the purchaser values the estate sale item, it is recycled and benefits another family. The estate benefits with unexpected cash and a freshly cleaned house.

Heirlooms left behind offer treasure-hunters the opportunity to acquire expensive items for little cost.

One way to fill your life with high-quality low-cost items is to shop estate sales, consignment shops, and second-hand shops. There are dozens of apps and websites that resell, so you may find treasure in someone's trash.

Currently, my style is Vintage Chic. For three years, I gave up retail shopping, and it opened up a new world. The quality and uniqueness of my clothes, gifts, and household furnishings exponentially increased.

Only occasionally do I now buy new. After the adventure of alternative buying approaches, "new" can seem a little boring!

Questions to Answer:

⊃ Have you tried any resale apps or website? If so, describe your experience.

⊃ Do you have items you no longer use? Would you consider selling or giving them away?

Reflection: Fund Your Priorities

For most people I know, spending is one of the biggest issues of life. How we spend tells more about who we are than perhaps any single fact about us.

> *Value-based spending is looking at your values first and budgeting accordingly.*

Value-based spending is looking at your values first and budgeting accordingly. If you uncover your purpose in life, you can more easily align your values and budget to support and fulfill that purpose. Value-based budgeting doesn't take a lot of money.

What it does require is intentional, consistent investment in what is important.

Remember, it's not how much you make; it's how much you spend—and where you choose to spend or invest your resources and finances.

Questions to Answer:

➲ How do you define your values?

➲ What would a look through your checkbook tell someone about you?

➲ Check at least annually to review what your finances tell you about your values

Reflection: Budget

Budgeting is essential for success.

I can hear you tensing up—this isn't everyone's favorite subject. But be assured that the more you do it, the easier it becomes. Now, with online tools, you have the convenience at your fingertips. We're actually highly privileged to live in a time when so many high-tech tools can help us be effective and prudent in life.

Still, I'll be honest. I don't like the process of budgeting. I simply know it's something very difficult for anyone to do *for* me and more essential to implement *for* me.

Here are some online resources that may help:

- www.mydebtfree.org is an excellent resource for beginners and those in debt or deficient payments
- https://www.personalcapital.com can be very helpful.
- https://christianpf.com/10-free-household-budget-spreadsheets. This website offers ten budgeting solutions for ten different scenarios.
- The mobile app called MINT gives you hands-on, assessible budgeting and fiscal management.
- Other financial curriculum includes: Financial Peace/Ramsey and Crown Financial.

Even though paper receipts are a thing of the past, take 30 days to print out your receipts. Keep them in a container or folder. Physically go through and sort and categorize your expenditures. Enter each expenditure under an Excel budget spreadsheet.

Review your expenditures and income to determine if you are in line with budget recommendations and your values and/or priorities.

Remember, if you struggle financially to save and/or are in debt, you may consider a program or class to help guide you toward fiscal stability. My recommendation is that you:

- Have an emergency fund for nine months with bare minimum living expenses.

- ⊃ Give 10-15 percent (at least 10 percent of gross income and revenue to your house of worship).
- ⊃ Save 10-20 percent (retirement and liquid cash).
- ⊃ Max out all retirement matches by your employer.
- ⊃ Pay down consumer debt, starting with the highest interest rate.
- ⊃ Have a will/trust/estate plan.
- ⊃ Rent or housing plus maintenance should be less than 30 percent of your income.
- ⊃ Keep transportation costs under 10 percent.
- ⊃ Limit utilities to about 2-4 percent.
- ⊃ Food depends on the size of your family and your lifestyle.
- ⊃ Entertainment is based on your disposable income.

Questions to Answer:

- ⊃ Do you have a budget? If not, Complete a budget for the next year.
- ⊃ Track expenditures for at least 30 days and preferably 90.
- ⊃ Having done so—what surprised you?
- ⊃ Does your budget reflect your values and priorities?

Reflection: Saving Ideas

Here are a few of my favorite savings ideas that have helped me (and others) propel to new levels of financial freedom and security.

- ○ Give generously.
- ○ Align your credit card with your lifestyle and stage.
- ○ Take advantage of travel perks.
- ○ Plan everyday purchases.
- ○ Fulfill cash-back opportunities.
- ○ Declutter your space and closets—resell access.
- ○ Move your body; clean your own house, mow your own lawn, or create a garden of fresh herbs and vegetables; wash your own car.
- ○ Go to the park.
- ○ Take good care and maintain your house, car, and other treasures and valuable assets.
- ○ Cook at home.
- ○ Invest systematically, regularly, and consistently.
- ○ Invest in diverse resources, broadly across the spectrum—seven to eight.
- ○ Shop estate sales and consignment.
- ○ Keep your car as long as you possibly can.
- ○ Make your gifts and cards.
- ○ Downgrade or cancel cable TV. Use streaming options, DVD, etc.
- ○ Rideshare, even with those within your home.
- ○ Become an entrepreneur and/or business owner.
- ○ Leverage the new tax laws. Know and understand laws and how they impact you. We are bunching our deductions/giving into one calendar year versus spending it over two or three. (Seek the advice of your CPA or tax advisor.)
- ○ Take advantage of loyalty programs/senior or AARP discounts.

> *Move your body; clean your own house, mow your own lawn, or create a garden of fresh herbs and vegetables; wash your own car.*

- Buy insurance: life and long-term care.
- Buy stocks when the market is low.
- Dollar-cost averaging investing (i.e. consistently purchasing set money each month).
- Establish Roth as Emergency Saving fund (over five years).
- Consign and/or sell treasures that are no longer needed or valuable to you.
- Consider quality over costs, prestige, or appearances.
- Become a minimalist or embrace simplicity as a goal.
- Join the sharing economy community. Co-op; warehouse, etc.
- Work hard.
- Buy refurbished/reconditioned products.
- Use sharing medical coverage like www.christainhealthcare.org
- Don't buy the Bentley when the Ford will get you there just as well. Instead, rent the Bentley and enjoy it for a special occasion.

Websites:
https://christandpopculture.com/less-minimalism-can-cant-teach-us/
http://www.hipdiggs.com/joshua-becker-christianity-minimalism/

Apps:

- OverDrive: free library
- Poshmark.com
- Let go
- Take a course that will enable you to learn to budget, save, and give while holding you accountable. Try Mydfree, crownfinancialministries, financialpeace.

Questions to Answer:

- Develop a plan to save more.
- What three steps will you implement from above?

LIVE YOUR MISSION

Reflection: Your Garden Flourishes

Today, I decided to go and pull all the weeds from my veggie garden. We had decided to grow our own garden.

Until today, I thought that perhaps the weeds were fresh veggie plants. Still, they produced no fruit—nothing. So, I reached in deep and pulled them out. The weeds were bigger and healthier than the veggie plants. Now the veggies may prosper!

Weeds are found in all kinds of gardens. The garden of our habits has weeds (procrastination; fast food). The garden of our emotions has weeds (bitterness; envy). And yes, the garden of our relationships has weeds, too.

Look around and identify the weeds in your garden. Cut them out! When you pull the weeds up, pull by the root. It may take a lot of effort and thoroughness. Some "friends" drain you intentionally; others are just toxic. Yet a few are imperfect people who are doing their best to survive. You might not be the help they need. Send them on their way gently, lovingly, and wishing them well.

Look around and identify the weeds in your garden. Cut them out!

After you have cleared the weeds, keep your soil (heart and mind) fertilized and benefiting from the sun and rain that nourishes your life.

Questions to Answer:

- Who in your life is a "weed"?
- Are you able to recall a situation where separation from a relationship left you healthier?

Reflection: Remind God of His Promises

Many of us are faithful, yet our lives appear to be at a standstill. There is no peace nor advancement. What's the problem? What should we do?

First, believe God and know he is a rewarder of those who trust him.

Second, stand on God's promises.

Third, make sure you're being obedient.

Fourth, discern what is truly going on.

Fifth, respond, knowing his promises are true.

Sixth, tell him through prayer what you hope for.

Seventh, thank God for the unseen result.

Eighth, encourage others who may doubt.

Ninth, understand that God's answered prayer may look different from what you expect.

Questions to Answer:

- Do you know what God's promises are? What will you do to find out?
- Name three scriptures you would like to remind God of his promises.
- Describe a circumstance where God's promise came true.

Reflection: Take the Time to Order My House

If I want to order my house—and, of course, I want to!—it all begins with setting a vision.

What do I want my "house" (my life) to be all about? What vision has God given me for why I'm here? What do I want to get done during the next year? The next ten years?

Then I must realize that time is a gift from God. He never gives any of us even the briefest instant less than we need. Nor does he give us more than we need. God gives us exactly the time we need to do exactly the tasks he has ordained. I need to take the time to understand his time.

Lord, thank you for the precious, anointed, and holy time you have given me to:

- ⊃ Reflect
- ⊃ Love
- ⊃ Organize
- ⊃ Study
- ⊃ Maximize investments
- ⊃ Build businesses
- ⊃ Exercise
- ⊃ Eat healthily
- ⊃ Mentor my children and other young adults
- ⊃ Optimize the Time
- ⊃ Seize the Moment and Appreciate it!

Questions to Answer:

- ⊃ What are the essential steps for you to create order in your life?
- ⊃ How will you maximize the moment?

Reflection: Be Vigilant

When we are alertly watchful, especially to avoid danger, we are vigilant. So then, let us not be like others, who are asleep, but let us be awake and sober.

1 Thessalonians 5:5-6 (NIV)

I love the word *vigilant*! It's the idea of a soldier at the outpost, wide awake, alert, and ready for danger. The soldiers may sleep in peace because the guard on duty is vigilant.

But vigilance doesn't have to be about guarding *against* something; you can also be vigilant in the expectation of something wonderful. Have you ever watched an eight-year-old during December? She is vigilant for Christmas. She will be ready when the morning arrives!

Jesus talked about those who wait for him. Talk about alert:

Keep your shirts on; keep the lights on! Be like house servants waiting for their master to come back from his honeymoon, awake and ready to open the door when he arrives and knocks. Lucky the servants whom the master finds on watch! He'll put on an apron, sit them at the table, and serve them a meal, sharing his wedding feast with them. It doesn't matter what time of the night he arrives; they're awake—and so blessed!

You know that if the house owner had known what night the burglar was coming, he wouldn't have stayed out late and left the place unlocked. So, don't you be slovenly and careless. Just when you don't expect him, the Son of Man will show up.

Luke 12:35-40

When we are alertly watchful, especially to avoid danger, we are vigilant. But can we be deceived?

Last night, I had a dream that a postman showed up at our door. He was tall, stately, the very image of a solid, trustworthy public servant. We didn't think twice about inviting him in. But in my dream, it was a bad decision. The postman walked all over our house breaking things, creating problems, doing harm. Maybe it was an odd dream, but for me, it was a kind of parable. I woke up with one thought: *Be vigilant.*

Later that day, I purchased some fresh veggie plants with my husband. We walked to the car. I'd placed my new spinach and romaine lettuce plants against the bushes, and a large, red spider crawled up my dress.

I ran out of the car in a panic, now unable to find the spider. I sat in the back because it still could be in the front seat! My husband spotted the thing. I knocked it out of the car and stomped on it. My husband asked me to make sure I killed it.

It was dead!

Be vigilant. Even among delicious veggies, there's bound to be a pest or two.

Questions to Answer:

- Describe a situation when you should have been more vigilant.
- How do you best determine a person's intent?
- Is discernment a legitimate ability, and will your "gut feeling" reveal the truth?

Reflection: Lessons from Lottie Mama

Years ago, we were enjoying our annual Christmas celebration family dinner. My grandmother, Lottie Mama, looked at my husband and me and said, with no explanation, "You and your children are going to be rich."

At the time, I was a stay-at-home mom with my children. We were living off the meager income of my husband's just-out-of-college job. Occasionally, my parents would chip in and buy our children shoes and coats.

I didn't understand her words, nor could I see how they could possibly come true.

Still, her words of hope and confidence in God resonated and stayed with me. Now Lottie Mama is with the Lord, and I'm sure she's looking down and saying, "I told you!"

True wealth, of course, isn't measured in dollars and cents. Peace, love, and hope for tomorrow are the currency that makes my life truly rich and abundant. However, we're on the path to building generational prosperity. We simply understand that humility, faith, and obedience will allow us to be better stewards of any funds we accumulate.

Thank you, Lottie Mama, for seeing what I could not see and having the faith in God to speak it over us.

Questions to Answer:

- Has someone spoken over you, and are you living in it?
- Are you speaking life into those around you?

Reflection: Rise and Shine

Rise and Shine!
Rise and Shine!
All hard-working men, fall out!
All hoboes, hit the road!
Rise and Shine!

When my dad was in the army, he used the hear the call above. Each morning, as I was growing up, he'd tell us, "Rise and shine!"

He had the best work ethic I've ever seen, and he demonstrated it in how he lived every single day. He expected nothing less from us, his daughters. I learned to enjoy hard work and take pride in the results.

Set your goals—go ahead and set them sky-high, if that's where you feel you should end up. Then get to work. It's not the height of your goals but the depth of your determination to work hard enough to get there.

Lazy hands make for poverty,
but diligent hands bring wealth.

Proverbs 10:4 (NIV)

Questions to Answer:

- How do you value hard work?
- Are there times when you can improve in this area?

Reflection: Smoke Alarm

One beautiful winter day, I loaded my fireplace with wood and a long, burning log. Because I was spending time writing and creating, I welcomed the ambiance of a warm fire.

Suddenly, smoke rose and filled the room and my house. My eyes were burning, and the smoke alarms began going off upstairs and down. The fire was creating a commotion!

I opened the windows to decrease the intensity of the smoldering fumes. My husband came home and handed me the fire extinguisher. Immediately I sprayed it on the log. Without warning, an explosion of white smoke filled my house. It was some type of chemical reaction—that's all I know.

As I gathered my senses and assessed the episode, I was grateful. Not one hair was singed. I looked around at my now smoke-filled home and gave thanks that nothing was lost. I also realized that every single bit of it belongs not to me but to God.

Everything in heaven and earth is yours. Yours, LORD, is the kingdom; you are exalted as head over all.

1 Chronicles 29:12

Question to Answer:

⊃ Share your life-threatening experiences and the lessons you learned.

Pillar IV: Be Radically Generous

You will be enriched in every way so that you can be generous on every occasion, and through us your generosity will result in thanksgiving to God.

2 Corinthians 9:11 (NIV)

You'd never guess where we got the word *generosity*.

It comes down to us from an old Latin word meaning, "of noble birth." What's that all about?

In the Middle Ages, *generōsus*, or *généreux* in Old French, described somebody who came from a wealthy or aristocratic family. Nobility was proven out by someone's willingness to give and to share wealth. But over time, more and more people began to notice the act itself rather than who was doing the acting. A generous act could be performed by anyone. It was the giving that made the biggest impression on people, not the relative wealth of that person.

Yet even today, when we see someone who is radically, abundantly generous, we think of that person as noble. Not of birth but of spirit.

117

In this Pillar, you will think about:

⊃ How to develop a plan to accelerate the change you want to see.
⊃ Situations where you have been loved despite yourself and your actions.
⊃ How you can be intentionally generous moving forward.
⊃ How you will be able to implement an abundance perspective.
⊃ What you're doing to focus on God, love and harmony.
⊃ What you need to stop doing and/or thinking to grow and to flourish.

DEFINE YOUR MISSION

Reflection: Be the Change You Want to See

Recently, my husband preached a sermon entitled, "Be the Change You Want to See." As I write these words, today is his birthday, so I choose to honor the way he lives his life by sharing the highlights of his message (though there are too many great ones to fit!).So many times, we look to others to change themselves or a situation. Instead, we need to look inside and be the change we want to see.

- ⊃ *Identify*: Close your eyes and reflect on how you want something changed. Is it a social ill or an upgrading of your economic status, so you may give more? Make sure it impacts your community and/or place of worship positively.
- ⊃ *Become informed*: Research and educate yourself on the topic.
- ⊃ *Link with others*: Seek a mentor, join groups, and/or partner with organizations that have your desire for change. Support, encourage or help implement the change.
- ⊃ *Set benchmarks*: Tasks, milestones and resources are key to reaching goals. SMART objectives: **S**pecific, **M**easurable, **A**chievable, **R**ealistic, and **T**imely apply here.
- ⊃ *Measure your progress* and recalibrate along the way.
- ⊃ *Hold yourself accountable*. Set deadlines.
- ⊃ *Celebrate success*.
- ⊃ *Be grateful* and tangibly say thank you!

Let me share a practical example: I wanted to share my gift of revenue generation and accelerating generosity with many, instead of just one organization. My plan was based on the points above:

1. Bring resources to nonprofits and churches.
2. Researched options from board membership to consulting.

3. Joined Generis, a Christian firm dedicated to accelerating generosity.
4. Challenged myself to learn the craft of consulting; built competencies and marketing systems. I consistently learn from others.
5. Recalibrated and repositioned myself.
6. Scheduled client fulfillment, marketing and outreach, mentoring. and business growth.
7. Took a trip to Mexico to reward hard work and have fun.
8. I thanked former clients.

Question to Answer:

⊃ Develop a plan to accelerate the change you want to see using the steps above.

Reflection: Abundance versus Scarcity

Thank God for his abundance!

Most of us are surrounded by abundance we fail even to acknowledge. Do you have a home? Do you expect your next meal to be freely available? Is there a beautiful, God-designed world all around you? Are there friends? Family members who love you?

What about the Word and wisdom of God? Are you able to own and read a Bible whenever you wish, soaking in ideas of power and goodness and blessing?

Try taking a day just to notice every good thing in your life that you can. Let your heart fill up with these observations until it overflows. Take the advice of Paul the Apostle:

Finally, brothers and sisters, whatever is true, whatever is noble, whatever is right, whatever is pure, whatever is lovely, whatever is admirable—if anything is excellent or praiseworthy—think about such things.

Philippians 4:8 (NIV)

What if fear has been keeping you from doing this? When we fear what is . . .

- Lacking
- Not done yet
- Not enough
- Under par

We miss the blessing!

Take the time to acknowledge, appreciate, express gratitude, and focus on what *isn't* lacking, what *is* done, what *is* enough, and what *is* above par.

Questions to Answer:

- Write about a scenario where your perspective influences your outcome.
- How are you able to implement an abundance perspective?

Reflection: Shalom

The Hebrew word *shalom* means to peacefully flourish. The root word actually meant *wholeness, completion.* Shalom is a sense of well-being and harmony within and without; the absence of agitation or discord; a state of calm that precludes anxiety or stress. In the midst of such wholeness, such inner and outer peace, you find you can flourish.

> *Shalom is a sense of well-being and harmony within and without*

Here are three ways to flourish:

⊃ Be loving. (1 Corinthians 13)
⊃ Be generous. (2 Corinthians 9:11)
⊃ Be purposeful. (Ephesians 2:10)

The result is harmony, joy, and salvation (Acts 2:42-47). And a wonderful cycle begins. While shalom encourages these wonderful actions—wonderful actions create a sense of inner peace. It's the opposite of a vicious cycle—a cycle of godly, joyful living.

You give love, you give generously, you give purposefully, and the inner peace that results causes you to give *more* lovingly, *more* generously, *more* purposefully.

Once you get that going, ordinary obstacles no longer stop you!

Questions to Answer:

⊃ Identify someone in your life you believe is flourishing.
⊃ What do they do that is different?
⊃ How may you emulate their path?
⊃ What actions do you need to *stop* doing and/or thinking to grow and flourish?

Reflection: More than Enough

Today, I read an amazing idea.

The Bible suggests there is a season of "more than enough!"

And Azariah the chief priest, from the family of Zadok, answered, "Since the people began to bring their contributions to the temple of the LORD, we have had enough to eat and plenty to spare, because the LORD has blessed his people, and this great amount is left over.

2 Chronicles 31:10

People were simply bringing their offerings—as we do every week—and the outpouring was so great, there was a fantastic abundance. In God's hands, there is always abundance. In the hands of Jesus, a boy's small lunch can feed a vast crowd.

We bring simple generosity; God brings the abundance. That simple mindset changes our lives in a radical way.

When we come from a perspective of *lack* or *little*, we act out of self-interest and manipulation. We cling. We hoard.

We must look at what we do have in our hands and realize they're in God's hands. Focusing on what is missing and comparing ourselves to others is both exhausting and counter-productive. Instead, celebrate what you have, be a good steward and be generous.

The disciples looked out at the crowd, saw 5,000 empty stomachs and thought, there will never be enough. Jesus immediately taught them that God is always more than enough. Five thousand people ate their fill, and there were leftovers!

All we need to do is willingly share what God asks us to share. Be grateful for what you have. Let him bless it, and it will exponentially increase in impact and provision. God gives us more than enough for our personal lives. You just bring the obedience.

Questions to Answer:

- ⊃ Do you focus on what you do not have?
- ⊃ Are you grateful for all that has been given to you?
- ⊃ How will you share your little to have a significant impact on others?
- ⊃ How are you adopting a "more than enough!" strategy?

Reflection: Scheduled Versus Important

I took off one morning to spend time with Dad and help my sister who broke her toe. We had so much fun.

As we were preparing for Dad's "school," he looked up at me with his deep-set, dark, round eyes and said, "I'm not going to school today."

"Why? The snow has melted."

He gazed at me as if to look past my face and into my soul, and he said, "Because I want to spend my day with you."

Wow! A parent who placed me at the top of his priority list; who told me every day that he loved me and our family more than any part of his life; who was never too busy to offer me an abundance of himself.

In other words, a father like our Father.

I thought I was past the days of "mommy guilt." Can I reach such a standard as a parent?

God-loyal people, living honest lives,
make it much easier for their children.

Proverbs 20:7 (The Message)

Questions to Answer:

○ Write about a time you've been flexible (or could have been) and put something important before something scheduled.

○ How did you feel about it afterward?

Reflection: Wagon Train

When we were young children, my twin and I would play with our sister cousins. Their mother died young, and they were being raised by my Grandmother, Lottie Mama.

One game was called Wagon Train. We'd jump on the beds, build tents, and prepare to go into the desert for weeks.

To prepare, we'd go down to my parents' refrigerator and pack food for the desert. My sister cousins would split up. Both always wanted to partner with my twin.

You see, my twin would pull all types of food from everywhere. She was very generous with our parents' food. On the other hand, I was a different story. I'd "conserve" and ration our food.

The sister cousin partnering with me would have meager bits of nourishment, while my twin had a smorgasbord. My mom explained later that whatever we had, my sister cousins could have; that there is *abundance* at our home and we were to share generously.

I thought I was being a good steward over my parents' resources. However, there was more than enough.

Share generously, and God will make the provision

Questions to Answer:

- When have you been hesitant to share?
- How will you adjust your outlook to be able to release unselfishly?

FUND YOUR MISSION

Reflection: Spiritual Vortex

Sedona vortexes (https://sedonaredrocktours.com/) seem to be powerful, transformational energy centers that are located at specific sites throughout Sedona, Arizona. Vortexes are the intersections of natural electromagnetic earth energy, also known as ley lines.

Ley lines can intersect in different ways, creating different types of energy vortexes. The three most common types of vortexes are magnetic, electrical, and balanced vortexes.

Here is a practical example of a vortex in my life. My husband and I were charged by our pastor to lead a campaign at our church. We had joined the church only the year before and did not know many of the people, yet our pastor insisted. We reluctantly agreed.

My job was extremely demanding and time-consuming, and my husband was just starting an entrepreneurial venture that took a significant investment of his time.

An even greater challenge was that my parents were ailing and had been hospitalized 12 times over the past year. The pressure was great in almost every area of our lives.

We wanted to stay under the radar as far as the church was concerned—at least on Sundays we could rest. God, through our pastor, had a different plan.

As we led the campaign, we matured and grew closer to God. We saw a transformation in the congregation. We taught families how to live fiscally responsible lives while encouraging them to be generous. There were "impossible" results in what God was doing under our leadership.

As the campaign was concluding, we made a major philanthropic commitment. It was the largest amount we had ever dared to give. We made a tremendous sacrifice (by our standard) to give that generously.

On our way to commit in front of all the leaders of the church, I received a call from my employer. I'd no longer be working there. We had started the business, and my husband had gone without income as he built its infrastructure.

So here we were, not only challenged to keep tithing at a significant level but to *expand* our giving to include this additional sacrifice. *Ouch!*

A couple of years later, we looked back. Miracle after miracle had come to pass. I was called to this work of generosity consulting. My husband's business took off, and he was also appointed to a church. We were able to pay off our commitment while increasing our tithes and offerings to God's church. We experienced a *spiritual vortex* only orchestrated by God.

Whether you've experienced a vortex or not is not the point. Our lives and particularly our finances and health experience transformational episodes that stay with us. Some call it lessons learned; others, miracles. It's those times when we unexpectedly encounter an intersection of factors that fit together to transform our situation. We cannot predict them nor cause them.

In the center of a vortex is *peace*; shalom. Stay still and enjoy despite the whirlwind around you.

Questions to Answer:

⊃ Write about a spiritual vortex in your life.

⊃ How did it transform you and your finances?

Reflection: Position Yourself

I shared earlier how we agreed to serve as campaign executive directors of our church's campaign to eliminate debt. Getting involved in such good work moved us to take the lead in sacrificially giving. And as usual, we reaffirmed a powerful truth: Those who give receive more from the act than anyone else. You can't outgive God, and he blesses our obedience in ways far richer than whatever sacrifice we made.

Why do we commit to give?

First, for victory in battle. My battles at that time included:

⊃ My parents being hospitalized 12 times
⊃ Accident: two surgeries and three procedures
⊃ Our dog Honey's terminal cancer and inevitable death
⊃ False accusations at work
⊃ Lack of work for husband
⊃ New business venture
⊃ Many smaller mistakes

Second, we commit for love of the church.

⊃ For the preaching of the Word
⊃ For the blessing of our congregation
⊃ For the warmth of fellowship

Third, we commit out of obedience to sacrifice.

⊃ Discipline to budget and not spend.
⊃ God's promise: Faithful over few things, ruler over much, Matthew 25:21

Fourth, we commit out of gratitude.

⊃ For spiritual elevation
⊃ For the new dream job that he provided
⊃ For going to my favorite city monthly

- ⊃ For debt-free living
- ⊃ For no new hospitalizations nor surgeries for parents or us
- ⊃ For growth and leadership
- ⊃ For health and wellness
- ⊃ For prospering business
- ⊃ For vacations awarded

Of course, these were only the beginning. After making this major fiscal commitment, we found that our lifestyle adjusted. The sacrifice became much less painful and even bought us joy. One of my mentors, Dr. Herman Norman, often says, "With sac-rifice comes joy."

"With sacrifice comes joy."

Questions to Answer:

- ⊃ Have you ever given generously and then experienced joy?
- ⊃ Stretch yourself. Do something outrageously generous.

Reflection: Generous Living

"Everyone will give an extra $400 if they can this year. That way we don't have to sacrifice."

Wait a minute: We don't have to sacrifice? As I read 2 Samuel 24:24, I understand the message that I will not offer God that which costs me nothing.

Then I think of Jesus' story of the widow's mite, in Luke 21:1-4. He said that all the others gave out of their wealth, but this woman gave all she had—and, therefore, it was a sacrifice, precious to God. We don't seek equal giving as the pastor above did; we seek equal sacrifice.

Sacrifice is an expression of faith. It costs us, and, therefore, we stretch ourselves, which means God can grow us. He can shape us into wiser, godlier creatures. He promises to reward our sacrifice and our generosity by enriching us in all ways. As 2 Corinthians 9:7-15 says, he will bless you "abundantly so that in all things at all times, having all that you need, you will abound in every good work." (NIV)

Asking everyone for the same sacrificial amount is not biblical nor practical. When my husband and I were paying for private college tuition exceeding half of our income, we could not sacrifice what we could do today with no tuition costs. God is a God of mercy and love. My heart aches for Christians that give generously and sacrificially, yet it may not reach the bar set by church leaders. On the other hand, those who do not have unexpected nor high expenses may believe they are champions because they gave what was asked.

Shaking my head: How did they come up with $400 anyway?

Questions to Answer:

ↄ Does your church take the "everybody give X" approach?

ↄ Do you expect everyone to give the same?

LIVE YOUR MISSION

Reflection: The Blessing of Generosity

Today, as we were leaving the grocery story, we noticed a woman also leaving. My husband held the door for her. He smiled and said, "Ladies First."

She expressed appreciation for his gesture of kindness. It turned out she was from Liberia. As we began to chat, she explained to us about the war there and how it impacted her community. Once, she said, some strangers came to town. The woman and her family fed the outsiders; they offered hospitality for them to come and refresh themselves.

Weeks later, the war had reached their land. The opposing faction ravaged the town and destroyed everyone except this woman and her family. The opposers protected the woman and her family and helped her go to another country. A simple act of generosity had saved their lives, even with evil people.

Being generous does so many more things than we imagine. It sets us up for protection, favor, and returned generosity beyond our imagination. Because of generosity . . .

You will be enriched in every way so that you can be generous on every occasion, and through us your generosity will result in thanksgiving to God.

2 Corinthians 9:11 (NIV)

What I've just shared is my favorite Bible verse: a promise that generosity leads to enrichment in life.

Questions to Answer:

⊃ How can you go out and practice an act of kindness today?

⊃ Look at the most generous persons you know. How have their lives been enriched?

⊃ How will you be intentionally generous moving forward?

Reflection: Look Out the Back Door

You may have noticed I have interesting dreams. Here's another one.

My husband and I had just arrived back home from vacation in my dream. We had a dog, a very large dog. She was at home, waiting for us, and she needed to go outside for a walk. We came inside and looked out back. We had a huge beautiful backyard, and as you walked into our home, we had open windows framing the view of the backyard.

In that backyard was an unusual scene. There was a kind of foxlike cat who was obviously infected with rabies. This wild animal kept screeching and bumping against the back door, trying to get in.

Also, in this odd, dreamscape of a backyard was a German Shepherd mix dog, who'd just delivered puppies. She was exhausted, thirsty, and weak. She ran out of milk to feed her puppies. These puppies were running around, trying to get milk from the mother who was obviously dehydrated, lethargic, and had no more milk to give.

The foxlike cat was going after the puppies, taunting them and also infecting the puppies; trying to destroy them.

I love dogs, so I was especially upset. The sad picture of lack and helplessness in the mother dog touched my heart. I wanted to open the front door, but then I saw the grimacing face of the foxlike cat. I paused.

The dream is like a parable. What are we to do when there are so many needs out there? Poverty and starvation, whether physical or spiritual, economic or mental. There are so many needs. Yet to keep afloat, we're trying to take care of our own household and ourselves.

Still, the puppies were so cute and harmless. I wanted desperately to help them and their mother, even as I feared the fox-cat's desire to get into my home. There was also my dog to consider. I called Animal Control, but they said they couldn't come for weeks.

The dream left my questions unanswered. But life is like that—we look at the needs in our own backyard, our community, and we feel called to act. We see those who need love and care. But then we realize we have needs of our own! What do we do? Shut the

we look at the needs in our own backyard, our community, and we feel called to act

blinds? Look away? There are no easy answers, but I offer these recommendations:

- ⟃ Be compassionate.
- ⟃ Be smart. Jesus said we should be as shrewd as serpents but as gentle as doves. (Matthew 10:16)
- ⟃ Be praying at all times.
- ⟃ Know what resources are at hand.
- ⟃ Seek advice from experts (Animal Control, in my dream).
- ⟃ Face your fear and be certain it's valid.
- ⟃ Realize you're not alone, seek help and join with others for a solution.

Questions to Answer:

- ⟃ What steps will you take, so you have the space to help others in need?
- ⟃ When have you felt overwhelmed by local needs and your desire to help?
- ⟃ What did you do?
- ⟃ What obstacles came your way?

Reflection: Position Yourself to Love

I was very disturbed by the action of another person—and that was my cue to respond in love, insisting on seeing things through a godly perspective.

Instead, I became angry, impatient, and cold. How dare I fail to show love, mercy, and grace?

As my child was leaving for work, I described my situation, "Mom," came the reply, "this is your opportunity to show love, accept people where they are, yet continue to use your talent to get things done. Expressing concern is important. Don't judge—just be helpful and be careful. Enjoy your day at home with no travel."

I resisted the advice at first. But it resonated with me, and now I can say it changed me forever.

Questions to Answer:

ↄ Describe a situation where you have failed to show love.

ↄ Share a situation where someone loved *you*, despite yourself and your actions.

ↄ Describe how you seek wise advice—even from those younger and less experienced.

Reflection: Love is All You Need

God gave me an epiphany this morning during my prayers.

I felt his still, small voice speaking to me in a wonderful way. "You passed the test, and I am well pleased," he said. "You loved my people where they are; you didn't judge. Instead, you showed acceptance and gentle guidance. Therefore, that person embraced you where you are."

If you have a child, you know what it feels like to be pleased and proud when your child had taken a strong step forward, doing the right thing when the wrong thing was so possible and so human. Nothing could keep you from embracing your child and saying, "I'm so proud of you!"

God does just the same when we come to the fork in the road and manage to choose the high road that he wishes us to travel. That's when we hear his voice and feel the warmth of his embrace.

It's one of life's most wonderful moments.

Questions to Answer:

⊃ Describe a time you chose to love versus doing what comes naturally or reacting.

⊃ How did you feel afterward? How do you think God felt about it?

Reflection: God's Alarm

This morning, I woke up to God's special music, the kind only he can create.

There were birds chirping and a breeze gently brushing the leaves in the trees.

That's my alarm clock now, a gentle nudge to arise. I'm reminded that the best things in life are the ones closest to God—whether nature, his children or his Word. As the sun comes up, I begin a new day with that mindset. Fresh in perspective and ready to accomplish what is before me, I fall to my knees in gratitude.

Ready to accomplish what is before me

As I meditate and pray, I hear from God and experience peace and calm. I pour out my needs and desires for the day, and he showers me with love and encouragement and special instructions for the coming hours.

I'm thankful to God for another day—each and every one is a miracle in itself, another note in God's special music.

Questions to Answer:

- How will you start your morning?
- For one week, start your day with gratitude and meditation. Record the results.

Reflection: A Matter of Perspective

I was dreaming about the abuse I received from my former supervisor. In the dream, my employer hired a supervisor between me and my current, mean-spirited supervisor. After the new one met with my first supervisor, she was very cautious around me.

My new supervisor moved me out of my current office, which had a beautiful scenic view and a private bathroom. I moved into the office intended for her. I agreed to this out of respect and to acknowledge her authority over me.

When I settled into my new office, I found this room to be better than anticipated: larger and with special nooks. As I viewed the potential two living spaces, I could now see things differently. Instead of just looking back, longing for my old office, I began to make the best of it.

Sometimes, we need to look around and take a fresh perspective

Sometimes, we need to look around and take a fresh perspective that is unbiased by preconceptions. We should also take the time to appreciate what we do have, rather than long for the past or another place and time.

I'm grateful and at peace.

Questions to Answer:

⊃ Look around you now. What about your situation brings you value?

⊃ Are you appreciating where you are?

Reflection: Family Feud

We were assembled in the ICU waiting room because my cousin was deathly ill. We were in a mode of prayer and reflection. Though we knew all things depend upon God, we wanted her to pull through, and we prayed for her strength and healing.

After much sharing of old stories, my cousin's sister told us that their siblings were feuding over the land they inherited. It had gone on for decades and was the source of discord and division. As I listened to this account, I felt sad and embarrassed that my family engaged in bitter arguments.

I thought about my sisters and me. We too engaged in fruitless skirmishes about nothing that truly mattered. When I think about the verse, "the love of money is the root of all evil," I must ask myself what cleaning up I must do in my life to focus on love and peace.

My mother, who at that time was in and out of hospice, in the last days of her life, would have been so hurt and disappointed in us. Do the things that divide us truly matter?

Questions to Answer:

- Think of a conflict in your life. What would have happened if you'd been gracious, generous, and prayerful?
- Why do we as mature adults, knowing the love and mercy of God, participate in such back and forth?
- What are you doing to focus on God's love and harmony?

Reflection: Full Bucket

When it comes to popcorn, I have advice for you. When handed a bucket full of the stuff, divide it up to share and eat later. Because if you munch a whole bucket, you'll upset your stomach. Believe me, I speak from experience!

You've heard the old line about our eyes being bigger than our stomachs. Why is that such an ingrained part of human nature? Something in us causes us to grab out of all proportion to need or appetite. We want to mark our territory and mark it as wide as possible, whether it's popcorn or wealth. Our houses are filled with stuff we felt we just had to lay our hands on during the whim of some moment.

My child likes to say, "Mom, why do you have to stuff the elevator?

My child likes to say, "Mom, why do you have to stuff the elevator? Don't you know it may crash?"

Yes, we're intended to be upward bound on life's elevator—heading heavenward toward growth and godliness. Yet, we "stuff the elevator" with non-essentials.

Are we blind to our own greed? Do we believe that greed won't change us and throw a shadow over our lives?

Questions to Answer:

- Why do we overeat, overconsume, and overindulge?
- Describe a time you've "stuffed the elevator."
- What is causing that tendency in your life?
- How will you prevent it?

Reflection: Living Beyond Ourselves

I participated in the signing ceremony of the establishment of the Harriet Tubman National Historic Park! What an honor to have some small role in the legacy of one of my greatest heroes. Harriet Tubman was a woman who escaped slavery and went on dangerous missions, one after another, to rescue others who sought to escape.

With Harriet Tubman going on the $20 Bill, her legacy of human dignity and freedom receives a larger audience, all over the world. We all receive inspiration from her story. Bishop Dennis Proctor leads the Board that oversees the Harriet Tubman Home in Auburn, NY.

No one knows what will happen tomorrow. We pray we might fully embrace Harriet's legacy. May God use us for the good.

Harriet found a way to extend her impact even beyond her lifetime: She left her land and estate to the African Methodist Episcopal Zion Church. Her generosity shows us that God can take a little and impact much. Read the story of Elisha and the widow, in 2 Kings 4. God is always multiplying what is available. He did that through Harriet Tubman, and he'll do it through us.

Harriet found a way to extend her impact even beyond her lifetime

Thank you, Harriet, for your philanthropic spirit and teaching us to live beyond ourselves.

Questions to Answer:

- How will you leave a legacy?
- What vision for a long-term impact has God given you?

Reflection: That's Enough for Me

When our children were younger and as they became teenagers, they dreaded being around Mom and Dad. We had to roll our eyes; we'd sacrificed a lot to pay for their education. We'd worked hard to ensure our lifestyle to support family, bonding, and to give to the kingdom of God.

At one time, we just had one car. That's difficult in a home with teenagers who are active in sports, theater, and church activities. Especially when both parents worked outside the home, we spent significant time in the car driving and picking up carloads. Our car was old and the CD player broke; it played only one song by Patti Austin, *That's Enough for Me*. We used to sing together, and after a while, we received so much joy simply from singing this song louder and louder and to each other. We bonded, despite our sacrifice.

It's one more example of joy emerging from sacrifice.

Question to Answer:

⊃ Write about sacrifices you've made that have in the end become joyful.

Reflection: Make an Impact

My son was on the fast track after graduating from college. He was chosen by a Fortune 500 company to be in their executive leadership program.

This program was for recent college graduates who had the potential and the desire to be the next generation of corporate leaders. Though his job was challenging, he did well and enjoyed learning and growing with the corporation.

Then came a tragedy in our family. Our eldest nephew was killed, and we were all in shock over it. Violence on the streets appeared to be rampant. Everyone said that something needed to happen. Everyone looked at the statistics and shook their heads. But what else could we do?

> *Everyone looked at the statistics and shook their heads*

My son, a man of action, examined his heart. It told him to leave the corporation and the fast track executive leadership program to become a probation officer. Though the attraction of Corporate America was lucrative and appealing, he said, "If black men don't take responsibility and do something about the killing of black men, no one else will."

He spent three years counseling, coaching, and guiding men on how to be accountable and turn their lives around. Many lives were transformed. My son realized that not all young men are as fortunate as he's been, with a stable, secure, upbringing.

Those of us who are blessed must reach back and pull others up—even if that requires sacrifice on our part.

Questions to Answer:

⊃ How have you used your talents, finances, and time to change lives radically?

⊃ What can you do to be the change you want to see?

Reflection: Generosity is the Lost key

Have you ever lost a car key? Nothing is more maddening!

Recently, I was meeting with a church leader. He was a little confused because he had lost his car keys. He explained that he had not *misplaced* them—he and his wife had looked everywhere; therefore, they concluded, the keys were lost; gone.

Generosity, you could say, works like that. We may have a destination: God-inspired vision. We even have the vehicles to get there. Still, generosity is necessary, yet it's far from a given in our culture. Therefore, we miss the opportunity to help our fellow brothers and sisters in the Lord to grow and live enriched lives. The *key* is to create a sustainable culture of generosity that spreads throughout our families and communities. Generosity is the lost key.

Toward the end of the meeting, my colleague received a call that someone had found his keys. He was overjoyed. I hope we find the generosity we seem to be missing.

Questions to Answer:

- ◯ How, exactly, is generosity the key as you understand it?
- ◯ Describe your journey to be generous and encourage others.

Reflection: Jesus' Last Week on Earth

One of my Generis colleagues spoke on Jesus' living example in his final week. You may never have thought of it this way, but that week was a sustained message of generosity.

Here is a summary:

- The widow gave her last. (Luke 21) Poverty.
- Mary anointed Jesus' feet with perfume. (John 12) Worship.
- Leaders gave a colt. (Matthew 21) Generosity of possessions.
- Upper room Passover meal. (Matthew 26) Generosity of hospitality.
- Jesus washed their feet. (John 13:4) Generosity of servanthood.
- Healing of the soldier's ear. (Luke 22) Generosity of mercy and compassion.
- A wealthy man gave his tomb. (Matthew 27) Generosity of possessions.
- Jesus' crucifixion. (John 19) Generosity of life.
- God gave his Son. (John 3) Generosity through sacrifice.

Jesus spent his last days illustrating the ultimate generosity. What better lesson for us that the greatest legacy comes through generosity?

Questions to Answer:

- Name three ways your life exudes generosity.
- Who in your life inspires generosity?
- Interview them and uncover their *why.*

Reflection: Thank You

Saying thanks doesn't cost a dime. However, *not* saying thank you may cost your church or nonprofit a committed member.

Many sacrificially give to support the church or nonprofit as well as to be obedient. But we could do a better job recognizing and expressing gratitude to those who have given.

> *Hearts and motives are not our territory; they're God's.*

But how do you know whether someone is giving sacrificially? Matthew 7 commands us not to judge others unless we want to be judged ourselves. So, we're not to decide on our own who gives the intentional widow's mite, or who gives pocket change out of a large base of wealth. Hearts and motives are not our territory; they're God's.

Here's what we *can* do:

- ⊃ Request everyone to pray about giving sacrificially, abundantly, and generously.
- ⊃ Showcase examples of how members and donors can change their lifestyles to give.
- ⊃ Show the impact of the gifts.
- ⊃ Just say thank you.

Frequently, personally, and sincerely express gratitude. Write a note. Even NBC's Tonight Show host, Jimmy Fallon, encourages writing those notes.

Questions to Answer:

- ⊃ How do you say thanks to your circle of influence? Your church? Your nonprofit?
- ⊃ What can you do to improve this personally and professionally?

Reflection: Altar of Remembrance

There are times in life when we do or experience something radical. It's a pivotal time of life change. We see things altogether differently. As a result, we're inspired to commit to doing better.

The "altar of remembrance" concept is biblically based. The Israelites in the Old Testament would stop and build an altar to commemorate a great act of God.

stop and build an altar to commemorate a great act of God

A corporate executive said he had a great job that he enjoyed. At the end of the year, he expected to earn a $30,000 bonus. He was as excited as any one of us would have been. In his mind, he started spending the money on various luxurious enticements. He didn't think about giving a portion to God through his church.

As the end of the year approached, however, it all turned upside down. Things were not going well at work. Weeks before Christmas, the company let him go without his bonus.

He was devastated and scared. His wife told him to give 10 percent of the bonus amount to the church anyway as an act of faith. Three thousand dollars, the amount it would come to, was a huge amount for such a young couple. He resisted the suggestion, but he prayed about it.

Through those prayers, he received a sense of peace and moved forward with giving sacrificially and generously to his church.

A few months later, he received a better job. And when the lost $30,000 was restored through his new work, he could only smile and give thanks to God. It was time for an altar of remembrance that he and his wife would never forget.

Questions to Answer:

⊃ What's your altar of remembrance?

⊃ How did it impact you?

⊃ Have you given sacrificially and generously?

Pillar V: Be Resilient

Consider it pure joy, my brothers and sisters, whenever you face trials of many kinds, because you know that the testing of your faith produces perseverance. Let perseverance finish its work so that you may be mature and complete, not lacking anything.

James 1:2-4

Now comes the testing ground.

Every good accomplishment in life demands perseverance; endurance; resilience.

The oak tree relies upon its strength, but eventually, the wind breaks it. The willow, on the other hand, learns how to bend, and even though it's thinner, even though it's less sturdy—it survives because of its resilience.

When life offers resistance, will you respond with resilience? Will you know how to bend, then return to your position?

In this Pillar, you will think about:

- ⊃ Who you know that inspires you, and why?
- ⊃ The characteristics of resiliency.

- ⊃ How knowing your purpose makes you able to withstand trials.
- ⊃ The choices you are making to live your purpose.
- ⊃ How you use quantitative factors to help make decisions.
- ⊃ The steps you will take to endure—to push through—despite the circumstance and obstacles.
- ⊃ How you heal from tragedy and loss.

DEFINE YOUR MISSION

Reflection: Riptide

As I swam in the ocean, my mind recalled my terrible riptide experience.

A riptide is a tide that moves in opposition to other tides, causing violent waters. They become strongest where the flow is constricted. So during an ebb tide, for example, as the ocean water is flowing back toward the sea, a riptide can come along with all its power and carry a person far offshore. An ebb tide at Shinnecock Inlet in South Hampton, New York, extends almost a thousand feet offshore. That makes a riptide very dangerous there.

When it happened to me, I was at the beach on a sunny day, safe and happy with the people I love. My teenage son, my nephew and I were jumping waves, laughing, clowning around. And just like that, we were ripped apart, thrown across the ocean into deeper waters.

we were ripped apart, thrown across the ocean into deeper waters

I fought with all my strength to keep my head above the surface, and I tried to push back toward the beach. But every time I came up for air, the turbulent waters sucked me back under. My son, seeing my distress, swam toward me, frantically yelling my name. I remember waving at him and yelling for him to go back to shore. I prayed; *God, please do not let my son see me die. Protect him and please do not let him swim toward these turbulent waters.* After being sucked under into the current like a rubber band over and over again, I collapsed.

My nephew, Andrew Troy Brown, saw I was caught in a riptide and being pulled farther into the ocean. (You will read about him later). He hurried to shore and called for the lifeguard, who quickly alerted

911 and came to pull me out. Without Andrew's quick actions and his willingness to seek help, I would not be alive today.

I was unconscious by this time, but the ambulance attendants revived me. Within a few hours, I was on my way back to normal health.

You may not have experienced a riptide in the ocean—if so, be grateful! Yet all of us experience riptides of other kinds in our lives.

Questions to Answer:

- ⊃ Describe a time you had an occasion when life threw you into helpless chaos.
- ⊃ Who helped you?
- ⊃ How did you survive or make it through?

Reflection: Does It Really Matter?

Sometimes in life, we're stuck on irritating yet insignificant matters. We lose our focus, our momentum comes to a halt, and we become consumed by some matter that seems urgent but, in the great scheme of things, isn't too important at all.

We hear this discussed in various ways. "Don't sweat the small stuff." Or, "Look at the big picture." My favorite way to say it is, "Keep your eyes on the prize." Push through, lock onto your goal, and don't let anything distract you.

Have you ever seen a horse pulling a wagon? They often wear blinders that prevent them from looking behind or beside them. Their gaze is, therefore, fixed on the road ahead, and they move forward. It doesn't work that way when you walk a dog, does it? The dog has no blinders. She'll enjoy inspecting every little item in the road, every bush, everything that comes into view. You have things to do, and you're eager for her to take care of business. But that's not her focus. Whatever is right in front of her is.

What distracts you? Is it some minor irritation? Address it with grace and dignity, always remembering that its real danger is pushing your *why*, your life goal, even farther into the future.

Questions to Answer:

⊃ Write down a scenario of everyday irritation and assess its true significance.

⊃ What can you learn from it to help you grow?

Reflection: Just in Time

As our franchise business and my church needed me, I transitioned from my job.

This was the time to build out the structure of our endeavor, the "bones," expanding our own reach and injecting profitability into our business.

Should I consult?

Become a CEO of a nonprofit?

Partner with my husband to become a business owner, instead of simply self-employed.

I explore what's in my heart—the vision God has placed within me. I realize I'm driven to become a social entrepreneur.

I actually made a decision chart to help me in the exploration process.

> I actually made a decision chart to help me in the exploration process.

This chart helped me weigh up my options and discern objectively and quantitatively what is best. My benchmarks were quality of life (QoL) issues, including financial implications, flexibility, using enjoyable skills, competency match, work environment, etc. Each QoL was given a weight (W) and multiplied by the Opportunity (OP) score.

	OP1	OP2	OP3	OP4
QoL1 W8				
QoL2 W2				
QoL3 W6				
Total				

Take me and use me was the prayer that undergirded this endeavor.

I joined Generis, a firm that guides churches and nonprofits in accelerating generosity. I was ready to be an entrepreneur.

Questions to Answer:

➲ What choices are you making to live your purposes?

➲ Are you exploring and weighing up the possibilities? How?

➲ How do you use quantitative factors to help make decisions?

Reflection: Openings and Cracks

My husband and I were in the backyard together. He noticed a *huge* black spider on the basement screen door. It was the biggest spider any of us had ever seen.

That screen door was broken and was ajar. The spider could have easily clung to the interior door when we opened it and come in. To my tremendous relief, my husband killed the spider. Yes, I realize spiders have their own purposes in God's creation. I know they're not evil. But I'm still not a fan!

Much more important than any particular creepy crawly thing is the lesson that came to mind on this occasion. There are doors cracked open in life; doors and seams that allow unwanted influences and problems to steal into life and bite us.

It's important for me to inspect my life regularly, just as I'd inspect my house, and make sure all those openings are closed.

Search me, God, and know my heart;
test me and know my anxious thoughts.

Psalm 139:23.

Questions to Answer:

- How do you search your life?
- What cracks do you know about right now?
- How can you be on the outlook to ensure your path is safe?

Reflection: 13 Reasons Why to have Joy in the Journey

Thirteen Reasons Why is a Netflix-based TV show about a teenage girl and why she committed suicide. Needless to say, it's deeply troubling, especially as we realize that adolescent suicide has spiked in recent years. The rates of teens admitting to suicidal thoughts have doubled during the last decade. Suicide is now the second-leading cause of death among adolescents.

With the cruelty often shown by other kids, particularly with cyberbullying, my heart goes out to our young people. I want them to know that God promises a better life, one where there is hope for the future. Below, you can see how the hope of God is all throughout Scripture.

there is hope for the future

God Offers Joy in the Journey:

1. Romans 8:28. "All things work for the good . . ."
2. Galatians 5:22. The Fruits of the Spirit include joy.
3. James 1:2. "Consider it pure joy . . . whenever you face trials."
4. Luke 6:21-23. When rejected, "leap for joy because great is your reward."
5. Psalm 30:5. "Joy comes with the morning."
6. John 16:21. A woman's pain in childbirth gives way to joy.
7. I Thessalonians 5:16-18. Be filled with joy; "give thanks in all situations."
8. Luke 32:8. With healing comes great joy.
9. Psalm 119:54. "Your decrees are the theme of my song wherever I lodge."
10. Esther 8:16-18. The people celebrate with joy, and others want to be like them.
11. Acts 8:7-8. Healing leads to contagious joy.
12. Luke 1:46-48 "My soul rejoices in the Lord," for he is mindful of humble servants.
13. Psalm 68:1-6. As we dance in joy, God deals with those who are evil.

I'm happy from the inside out, and from the outside in, I'm firmly formed. You canceled my ticket to hell—that's not my destination!

Psalm 16:9-10 (The Message)

I take courage from the women in my life who have shown us why we should have joy in the journey:

Harriet Tubman led hundreds of slaves to freedom through the "Underground Railroad." The principles in the Scripture passages above can be found as you study her life. In the midst of our nation's darkest period and deepest sin—the sin of slavery—she created joy for others.

Mrs. Fannie James was a member of my childhood church. She would dance joyfully each Sunday and praise God sincerely, despite the circumstances of her life at the time.

Connie Palmer was another faithful follower of Christ, joyful and loving. She praised God through music and song, despite a cancer diagnosis. She insisted on being an encourager.

Malala Yousafzai is a Pakistani activist for female education and the youngest Nobel Prize laureate. Like Harriet Tubman, she turned weeping into dancing.

Questions to Answer:

- Who do you know that inspires you? Why?
- What are the characteristics of resiliency?
- Describe a time you had to be resilient.
- Where did you find the strength?
- How does knowing your purpose make you able to withstand trials?

Reflection: Release the Balloon

I've mentioned one of the most tragic moments of my life, the loss of my dear nephew, Andrew Troy Brown, MBA, LSS MBBC. I still mourn the terrible loss of someone so close.

Andrew was at the pinnacle of his life. He was about to marry the love of his life, who he met while the two of them were completing their MBAs. Andrew purchased a beautiful home on a golf course, received a fantastic promotion, and was one of the youngest Master Lean Six Sigma Black Belt Certification instructors in the country. Andrew was a member of Omega Psi Phi Fraternity.

Then, in the midst of so much blessing, came the car crash—and he was gone.

This is what Andrew posted on his LinkedIn page:

My goal in life is to help people be the best they can be. I try to live by a few simple yet powerful principles discovered by those wiser than I am.

My goal in life is to help people be the best they can be

- ⊃ *"I don't care who gets the credit; I just want to win."*
- ⊃ *"If you don't have time to do it right, when will you have time to do it over?"—John Wooden*
- ⊃ *"Be a blessing to someone."—Mom*
- ⊃ *"And now these three remain: faith, hope and love. But the greatest of these is love" (1 Corinthians 13:13, NIV).*

He continued:

We are all blessed with various gifts and talents, but I truly believe we're called to love and support our fellow man. I could bore you with my technical qualifications, which are listed below (wink, wink), but I believe the WHY is far more important than the WHAT in terms of living a purpose-driven life. I don't know exactly where life will take me, but I do know when it is all said and done, I want to hear, "Well done, my good and faithful servant." #OperationBeBlessed

Andrew was one of the most charismatic, intellectual, and amusing people I ever met. His death crushed our family. For what would have been his 30th birthday, I was leading an orientation session. One of the students spoke about his mother and how he releases balloons on her birthday each year.

This idea resonated with me. After sharing the idea on social media and text, Andrew's family and friends gathered across the country to release balloons in unity, honoring the memory of Andrew Troy Brown. We each wrote a personal note to Andrew and attached it to our personal balloon.

We watched the sea of purple and gold balloons escape into the heavens. Even though there were tears, we were able to feel joyful in the acknowledgement that God gave us the experience of knowing such a powerful force. Peace came upon us, and we knew all was well. It was the kind of cathartic experience of release that only God can provide.

Questions to Answer:

- ⊃ What experience in your life has been wonderful but too short?
- ⊃ Where do you need to release the balloon?
- ⊃ What steps will you take to endure—*push through*—despite the circumstance and obstacles?

Reflection: Flip Strategy

You intended to harm me, but God intended it for good to accomplish what is now being done.

Genesis 50:20 (NIV)

Bad things happen; no one will argue that point. But are you capable of taking the bad events—even the bad events that are intentional on someone's part—and lean into them to make them positive? If so, you have a "super power" to carry through life.

Negative events occur for all kinds of reasons. Sometimes, they're directly part of God's program for increasing our wisdom, growing us up.

Consider it pure joy, my brothers and sisters, whenever you face trials of many kinds. Because you know that the testing of your faith produces perseverance, let perseverance finish its work so that you may be mature and complete, lacking nothing.

James 1:2-4

I was brought onto Morehouse College to head up major gifts and serve as campaign director. God blessed my work tremendously, and many took notice. After just six months, I was promoted to Associate Vice President. My colleagues, who previously were my peers, were now reporting to me. Even though there had been resistance by a couple of my peers, the promotion revealed a few ugly emotions. They were furious and took out their wrath out against me.

I was no victim, though. With determination and focus, I forged ahead. In that process, my actions communicated that I only cared about results and not them personally.

My colleagues needed and deserved love. Yet I was focused on achieving goals and propelling Morehouse to new levels of resourcing.

My gifts were being maximized, and I too was astonished by growth in giving at the college. It was definitely a team effort.

One of the most outstanding results was to solicit and close the first $1 million cash gift to Morehouse from an alumnus. God gave me favor with the donors, the alumni, the students, and the professors.

The two colleagues, however, sought to set me up for failure. As with Joseph and his brothers, what they intended negatively, God used positively.

The experience taught me a valuable lesson. *Love first.*

Other lessons included, *listen to your gut and don't be naïve.* Envy and jealousy can become vicious—address them head-on. Do not let things fester.

Question to Answer:

⊃ Are you able to share a scenario where a negative occurrence eventually proved to be for your good?

Reflection: God is Our Source

The other day, I listened to the testimony of a church colleague.

For over a year, she'd been tormented at her job by her new supervisor. She didn't like the work; however, she was really good at it, and it paid well. Previously, the leadership was encouraging and had a partnering mindset. Now, with the new supervisor, there was disrespect and a condescending attitude. Given the combination of not enjoying her work and the harshness of the leadership, she knew she had to leave.

She soon discovered the job was a resource and a security blanket. She was offered a part-time position doing work she would enjoy. Still, the compensation was much less, both in benefits and in income. She measured the pros and cons, prayed over it, and decided to resign and take the leap.

Now she has the freedom to pursue entrepreneurial ventures and to work part-time doing enjoyable work and impacting young adults (her passion.)

As she said, the job is the resource—however, God is the Source. This experience helped her exercise her faith and move out of her situation of bondage and unfulfillment.

One word of caution: Being uncomfortable isn't always a sign you're in the wrong place. God does place us in such positions so that we may learn, grow, or acquire a skill. Being stretched and maturing are good things. Be prayerful about your circumstance and consider the costs before taking the leap.

Questions to Answer:

- ⊃ When have you depended fully on God's provision? What about now?
- ⊃ Describe a time when you took a leap of faith.
- ⊃ What is your passion?

Reflection: Who is the Boss?

And now, a word from Mom—her advice to wives and aspiring wives:

"Let the man know he is the boss. He has the final say. As wives, we are his respected advisors. Giving us what we desire makes our husbands the hero of the story. It also gives them the opportunity to love us.

"In the end, the best decision is made for our good, and most likely, it's within our own heart's desire."

So, really, looking at the big picture—who's the boss?

We are!

Questions to Answer:

⊃ Do you believe that men and women have different roles in relationships and marriage?

⊃ Was Mom talking about how to navigate upward? Explain.

⊃ How can we take advice from our elders that applies today?

Reflection: A True Story Continues

Way back at the beginning of the book, I told you about my husband's first experience flying First Class—and how he ran into Sean, our buddy, who was in coach. Sean's story continues to play out in fantastic ways.

He started a new, innovative entrepreneurial venture that will propel medical treatment to new levels of accessibility and effectiveness.

Sean shared with me that he grew up very poor. Born to teenage parents, he experienced a tough childhood on the mean urban streets. Still, he was gifted and focused. Sean feels blessed to be given this mantle. He speaks with youth and encourages them that they can succeed, despite their own circumstances.

Sean said there were several reasons for his success. One is that God planted many people in his path to encourage and help him. Sean credits his grandmother, good friends, his teachers, and his college for helping him through. There were life-defining moments along the way that helped him grow and evolve to what God wanted him to be.

Sean came from a disadvantaged background and soared. He and his family continue to live a First Class Life.

Through Sean's life, we can see the five pillars of a First Class life:

- Be Disciplined.
- Be a Masterpiece.
- Be Diligent.
- Be Radically Generous.
- Be Resilient.

Questions to Answer:

- What defining moments helped to shape you?
- How will you live a First Class life?

FUND YOUR MISSION

Reflection: Double for Your Trouble

One of my new colleagues told me about the death of her four-month baby boy. I wept with her to hear such a heart-rending life story.

Within weeks, she was pregnant again—this time with twin boys. They are 11 now. She will always miss her baby boy. He will live in her heart forever. But she can offer even deeper love and appreciation to the two twin boys in her life because of what she went through.

God gives us double for our trouble. There are times in life where we must sacrifice and give, whether it's losing sleep over a child, or making a generous financial contribution.

My husband and I made a generous, sacrificial commitment to our church above and beyond our regular tithes and offerings. We had three years to fulfill it. We decided, among other lifestyle changes, to reduce our vacations from two weeks a year to one week.

The money we'd spend on the second vacation was given as part of our fiscal commitment. Within 60 days of deciding to make the sacrifice, we received a notice that there was a class action lawsuit against our timeshare exchange company. They rearranged our agreement.

Now, instead of one timeshare vacation per year, we can take up to four into perpetuity. Yet our cost remained essentially the same.

Double—or more—for our trouble. Life is tough, but God is full of wonderful surprises when we're obedient.

Questions to Answer:

- Describe a time you received double for your trouble.
- Did you credit him for it at the time? How can you express your gratitude now?

Reflection: Taking Up Space

It just had to happen. My oven malfunctioned hours before I was to host Thanksgiving Dinner.

Last night, as my child and I were preparing Thanksgiving dinner, in particular, the turkey and the quiche, the new oven shut off from its preheating state. The stovetop worked fine. I didn't panic but made several unfruitful attempts to revive it.

No success.

So why *now*, when I most needed the oven? We were expecting 30-plus hungry guests. My new kitchen was poised to be showcased. This was my first extended family event.

I stopped, reined in my emotions, and reminded myself that God is in control of everything, including my oven.

Lesson: Something may look great, be expensive, and beautiful. My new oven was all of those things. Still, if it does no good, it's just taking up space.

Questions to Answer:

⊃ Have you assessed what "shiny things" are taking up space in your life and finances?

⊃ Do you have an account, investment, or property that occupy space yet aren't producing revenue nor growth? How can you fix it or discard it?

Reflection: Eat the Fish and Spit Out the Bones

The saying above is so true! Still, it's from the olden days, when there were so often bones throughout your fish. Fillet of fish was rare. The fish was tasty, yet our eating experience was disrupted by spitting out these little bones that could potentially be caught in your throat.

It was hard to enjoy the taste as much as you wanted because you had to be on guard with every munch. If you talked too much or didn't pay attention, a bone could become stuck in your throat and make you gag. Many people refused to eat fish because of the experience.

Life is that way, and finances are no different. Sometimes, you have to "chew with care," sort through the bad to devour the good. This could mean budgeting for expenditures in advance, balancing your account, or denying yourself a desired commodity. If you take the time to spit out the bones, you will have a smooth and satisfying eating experience.

Sometimes, you have to "chew with care," sort through the bad to devour the good.

Investing the preparation time ahead will benefit you in the long term.

Questions to Answer:

つ What "bones" should you be spitting out?

つ When you are short-term focused, what happens?

つ How can you position your finances, so they benefit you and create a "tasty" experience?

LIVE YOUR MISSION

Reflection: Paris is Always a Good Idea

What was the most eye-opening trip you ever took? What experiences there changed you forever? Travel has a way of doing that.

When I was in college, I studied French as a minor. I excelled academically and was offered the opportunity to study abroad in Paris, France. The experience altered me forever.

Since then, I have always treasured Parisian things. My eldest child gave me a journal book entitled *Paris is Always a Good Idea*. Many of my writings actually started in that journal. I will never argue with the suggestion that Paris is a good idea because it certainly was for me.

When I think of Paris or describe my experiences there, my face lights up. Friends see the joy it gives me. The beauty of the city, the romance of the French language, the memories of that time of my life—graduating valedictorian from college, marrying my husband, and starting a career and family.

Paris is my happy space, and the very thought of it helps me pull through life's ups and down.

Questions to Answer:

⊃ Write about an experience that brings you joy, even though it may have been years ago?

⊃ What do you do to rest and to take a break?

⊃ Where does your mind go when you need a "happy space" to calm down or fall asleep? Why have you chosen that subject?

Reflection: On Va La Vie

I'm a twin who spent the first part of life with my sister by my side—then met my husband as soon as I went to college. *Alone* is not something I do! I'm as much of a "people person" as anyone can be.

So, I was terrified—absolutely terrified—on that occasion when I went overseas to study French in Paris, France.

The city was beautiful, and it was all like a dream, but still, I longed for the comfort and familiarity of home: a single, loving smile, a knowing gesture. The language barrier was real. Parisians were cold and didn't appreciate Americans.

Here's what it was all about: God wanted me for himself. I'd spent enough of life being people-dependent. He sent two angels from the states—Audrey and Jessica—to show me the way. As I guided them through the nuisances of Paris, I was grateful for their presence. But they gently pointed me toward Christ.

*God wanted me for himself.
I'd spent enough of life
being people-dependent.*

One evening, I was alone, and God spoke to me. Satan wanted control of my life—I could feel him hovering, yearning for the ruin of my soul. God tenderly loosed Satan's grip on my body and life. I accepted God as my savior and couldn't stop thanking him for coming into my heart. At 19 years old, a different human being went home to America from the one who had left there.

True joy comes from living your life for Christ—allowing Him into your heart and trusting him completely. Paris is where I met Christ and accepted Him into my life, my Lord and savior.

Have you accepted Jesus as your Lord? If not, read on. This next part is just for you.

God is calling to you this moment, and there's no reason to delay. Here is a simple prayer you can offer.

Dear Jesus, I believe you are Lord and control everything. Please forgive me for all I have done that is wrong. Come into my heart and guide me in your path. Show me how to live an abundant life. I believe you died for my wrongdoings. Thanks for loving me. Thanks for saving my soul. In Jesus name.

Now, go and tell someone—a church leader—a wise Christian friend—you are saved and a child of God!

Questions to Answer:

⊃ If you already trust Christ as the master of your life, how is he guiding your daily decisions?

⊃ If you're unsure about committing to him, what are the obstacles?

⊃ How can you learn more about being a Christian?

Reflection: Wisdom in Mishaps

I'll be honest. These past few days have been a battle.

From all the mishaps, I've gotten some solutions. One is to catch the mishap early. Take stock of your situation. Identify what exactly is happening and why. There are always lessons.

- Learn
- Prepare
- Watch
- Pray
- Plan
- Do not hoard
- Rest

✓ Saturday, my beloved Audi car engine died.

✓ *Lesson: Plan for the unexpected.*

✓ I gave the car to a university.

✓ *Lesson: Look to do good from a bad situation. Be generous.*

✓ My dog Honey's back right leg patella tore, requiring immediate surgery. She had been doing a lot of jumping from one level of the yard to the next.

✓ *Lesson: Pay attention. Be prepared.*

✓ My inexpensive kitchen cabinets were too full. They came crashing down, breaking 70 percent of our dishes. They'd been overcapacity in the space allotted.

✓ *Lesson: Watch for overcapacity. Trim the fat.*

✓ I needed a second shoulder surgery as I didn't heal properly.

✓ *Lesson: Rest in God; slow down.*

✓ My child's car was broken into.

✓ *Lesson: Secure treasures.*

✓ My husband is scheduled for knee surgery . . . My child was fired for a trivial reason.

✓ *Lessons: Stuff happens. Exercise wisdom.*

✓ *One last lesson: Victory finally comes. Thank God for it!*

Questions to Answer:

⊃ Have you had a series of mishaps?

⊃ How do you handle the pressure?

⊃ What lessons did you learn?

Reflection: Circumstances Reveal You

My eldest sister is a pastor. She was selected to preach at the annual church conference with over a thousand attendees. Her sermon title was "Between a Rock and a Hard Place."

Godly leadership, she said, requires us to:

- ⊃ Accept that we are in a constant, lifelong struggle against our own humanness.
- ⊃ Acknowledge that only through utter dependence on him will we be in God's will.
- ⊃ Ascribe all positions, places, and power to God

My sister preached:

"We know there will be obstacles as well as opportunities; there will be triumphs as well as grief—yes, rocks and hard places.

"But there is good news for us, the New Testament leaders, for we are given not only instructions by God, but we are allowed through the mercy of God a chance to benefit from the presence of the Holy Spirit in our lives.

"Challenges will come; opposition will raise; naysayers will talk. But God is present. We have confirmation of this Scripture truth:

Remember our history, friends, and be warned. All our ancestors were led by the providential Cloud and taken miraculously through the Sea. They went through the waters, in a baptism like ours, as Moses led them from enslaving death to salvation life. They all ate and drank identical food and drink, meals provided daily by God. They drank from the Rock, God's fountain for them that stayed with them wherever they were. And the Rock was Christ. But just experiencing God's wonder and grace didn't seem to mean much—most of them were defeated by temptation during the hard times in the desert, and God was not pleased.

1 Corinthians 10:1-5 (The Message)

At that time, as she preached these words, my sister had just lost her husband of 36 years. Also, her employer restructured, and her job was eliminated. Then, the following year, my sister lost her son through a tragic car accident. My sister had every reason to withdraw into a hole.

Yet, despite all these trials, she persevered and survived.

I didn't know my sister was that strong. Or that anyone could be that strong.

When you witness up close the resilience of others, you receive fresh inspiration to seek that same strength. It's available in Christ.

Questions to Answer:

⊃ What circumstance revealed your true character?
⊃ What about you was revealed?

Reflection: Bitter Sweet

*My grace is sufficient for you, for my power
is made perfect in weakness.*

2 Corinthians 12:9

Today, my youngest child shared with me the bittersweet departure he had from training on his new job. He'd accomplished a major milestone and was glad the "bootcamp" was over. However, he bonded with some great colleagues and had fun. They became friends and didn't want their time together to end.

Yet they had accomplished their goal, achieved what they were sent to do, and now it was time to separate and go forward in their careers. They supported each other all along and have pleasant memories that only they could share.

> Life is filled with "bootcamp" experiences.

Life is filled with "bootcamp" experiences. Is mine ending? Have I graduated?

When I look at why Honey, my dog, passed away at such a young age, it's similar to my child's experience, if I look at it in a certain way.

Honey and I bonded quickly, supported each other, loved each other—so many good memories and fun times. I thought there would be many more years of this blessing.

I look to heaven and ask, "Why God? Why?" And I think I've received my answer.

Honey had accomplished what she set out to do. Her time with us had ended. She had accomplished her goal, achieved what she was sent to do, and now it was time to separate.

The Scriptures are clear:

God is Grace is enough. Unless we are weak, it is hard to depend on God's power. I'm so glad his power is made perfect in weakness.

Dear Lord,

Please make me whole.

Restore my joy; give me peace.

Remove the sadness; restore in me a glad heart.

Thank you, God, for answering my question of why, and giving me so many beautiful memories to cherish. I smile just to think of them. Help me to think on the gift, not the loss.

Questions to Answer:

⊃ Think of a person or animal you lost who was dear to you. How did you recover?

⊃ How was that relationship a gift?

⊃ What made that person special?

⊃ How are you able to carry that on?

Reflection: Healing and Restoration

This morning, I texted my supervisor and spoke into his life. My supervisor lost his home in a hurricane. He also caught the flu twice.

Sometimes, to be healed and to be restored, you need to be sick and almost destroyed first. Why has this horrible occurrence happened in his life? How does he pull through? He once told me he is a Christian; it was a simple comment, but he never mentioned it again.

This morning, I will pray that God's healing and restoration occur in his life as it has so many times in mine.

This year is my year of healing and restoration. Maybe God can, therefore, use me to help others along. So often, I've found that praying and encouraging others will help pull me through in the times when I need it myself.

Questions to Answer:

⊃ Has someone ever comforted you despite their own situation? Have you ever been ministered to by a "wounded healer"?

⊃ Have you ever encouraged someone, even though you may have been suffering yourself?

Reflection: Life on Pause

As I leave one job and go to another, my life is on pause. I'm in one of those odd places in life, where I'm neither here nor there. I'm ahead of the past but behind the future. What do I do?

First, perhaps I can realize that nothing is really different. We always live in this moment, the present. The past is always in our rear-view mirror, and the future is never quite what we expect.

> *The past is always in our rear-view mirror*

So, I can be excellent where I am; bloom in this tiny plot of soil. Do the things I've always wanted to do but never had the time. Plan for success.

Spend extra time connecting with God; reach out to an old friend. Reflect. Take stock.

And finally, build a bridge between growth and sustainability. It should involve:

- Solid Infrastructure
- Targeted Opportunities
- Fearless Launch
- Nurturing Relationships
- Smart Business Systems
- Innovative Culture
- Excellent Delivery

Questions to Answer:

- When have you experienced an expected time off?
- What did you do with the time?
- What can you do in this moment, the present, to maximize it?

Reflection: Looking Different

This morning, I was going through TSA (Transportation Security Administration). It's usually a quick process. But this morning, I was stopped, and the TSA agent questioned my appearance. He pointed out that I looked different from my license photo of two and a half years ago.

Yes, I'd changed my hair color, style, and wore it natural instead of straight—different texture, wearing glasses, weight gain, tan, etc. Yes, I could see why he questioned the ID picture. But there was more to my looking "different."

The photo on my driver's license was taken the Monday after we buried my nephew, Andrew, who was tragically killed in a car accident. Right before his death, I had surgery and lost a lot of weight. Also, my new career suffered as a result. My first-born child had a significant life-altering change that grieved me.

My twin and I were at odds regarding our aged, sickly parents' care. *Then* my husband was diagnosed with cancer. It was one of the saddest and most stressful times of my life. Literally *and* figuratively, it was winter.

Today, I've pulled through. I've fought the good fight, and I'm healthy and in good spirits. So is my husband. It's summertime—literally and figuratively.

When I look at the license photo, I revisit the Me of two and a half years ago, and I feel the pain of that wilderness period of my life.

When tragedy visits—and you know it will—take the time to heal and recover.

When tragedy visits—and you know it will—take the time to heal and recover.

Use the storm of life as an opportunity to change your "look." Reorder and reprioritize. Examine your values. Lean in to what is important. Align your lifestyle and finances to lay the foundation of where you strive to be. Be strong and courageous, know God is with you, and that this too will pass.

Questions to Answer:

⟳ When you have a tough time and pain in your life, do you get stuck?

⟳ What steps do you take to forge ahead?

⟳ How do you heal?

Reflection: Deep Sadness

Today I feel deep sadness—pain, hurt, fear, and disappointment. It's as if I'm carrying someone else's burdens, their load. Yet I don't know *whose* load; I simply feel it.

God will reveal the truth in time. My heart is breaking for someone I can't even name, and all I can do is pray.

Strongholds are being broken. I often carry the pain of others; however, these episodes are increasing both in frequency and intensity.

I know where I can start. There are people all around me who can use a little prayer—always. So, I lift up several situations I know about, and ask God to intervene in those that are not so apparent.

This has helped me think about everyone I know and be more observant about the lives of others instead of simply my own. Thank you, Lord, for making me your instrument of intercession and peace!

Questions to Answer:

- Have you carried someone else's load?
- Do you pray for others?

Reflection: Fresh Perspective

The Lord put on my heart not to focus on *stuff*. He's growing me up and helping me to put things into perspective. Life is so much more than possessions!

One of my family members is often belittling and mean-spirited. Still, it affects me differently than it did before, as I developed this perspective. However, they mean well. I try to focus on what is good.

Mom and Dad's caregivers' schedule had a couple of disruptions. It irritated me as I planned in advance. I had to take off from work unexpectedly. I was focused on prevention and use of time to undo what I had checked off as done.

As I was acknowledging the challenge, God used the situation to mature me to become more flexible and spontaneous. A terrible item of information came across the newsfeed.

Randomly, at a NYC subway system station, a man was pushed in front of a train, which crushed him. His wife witnessed the whole incident.

Immediately, I no longer had the luxury of caring about my relatively tiny concerns. My heart and prayers went out to the wife and family who had experienced unthinkable tragedy.

It is a matter of perspective, isn't it?

How many of the anxieties that truly consume us are worth the worry we give them?

Questions to Answer:

ↄ Describe a time when you lost your way and your perspective on what is truly important.

ↄ List your five leading anxieties and assess whether they're worthy of your stress.

Reflection: Cultivate Your Garden. Avoid Distractions

Do not text me. Please understand.

Our lives are full of distractions that knock us off course. How does this impact our capability to give? The greatest gift we can give to anyone, and more essentially to God, is ourselves. When we are pulled here and there, to and fro, we lose focus and are less able to accomplish our purpose. We're like little boats on a stormy sea, and we lose our compass.

Once, I was presenting to a client. I had my iPhone next to me. First, it was my time-keeper. Also, my phone has a Bible application where I've bookmarked essential Scriptures. While that's a great tool, it forced me to look at my phone throughout the presentation.

Still during this presentation, an intense public exchange, I received a text message. The message was critical and trivial. My heart was hurt, and my confidence took a quick hit.

The text's impact at this anointed moment was grave. I was thrown completely off course during a time I needed to exhibit confidence, boldness, and peace.

> *meditate on worthy, good, beautiful things*

Philippians 4 commands us to meditate on worthy, good, beautiful things. Negative, petty words are the opposite of that. Too often, we allow our tech tools to distract us and throw us off course.

> *Too often, we allow our tech tools to distract us*

So, I asked the sender to no longer text me, and I moved the text feature from my main screen. This person lost the privilege of texting me because of the lack of respect.

Even though you want those close to you to communicate, it must be done in love and in a way that cultivates your garden.

Our hearts and souls need cultivation if we're to soar.

Questions to Answer:

⊃ What will you do to stay on task and avoid distraction?

⊃ How do specific distractions prevent you from doing your best?

⊃ Do social media, chats, instant messenger or texts stop your flow of positive energy?

⊃ What steps will you take today to make your days more positive?

Reflection: The Cyst of Life

Many family members and friends questioned if I was okay.

They saw I was round in the middle, almost as if I were pregnant. I blamed it on menopause. However, dieting and exercise made no difference. My middle just expanded onward.

I was beginning to feel sluggish and tired. I was coughing violently. Finally, a family friend told me to check it out with a physician. More than the large middle, the cough was disruptive to my work and sleep. After a month of tests and doctor visits and explosive growth in my middle, the specialist diagnosed me as having large cysts. Tests revealed they were not cancerous, thank God.

Still, the cysts were growing rapidly and causing pain and discomfort. My stomach was far larger than is normal for me. I focused on getting better.

I was hospitalized for a week and had extensive surgery to remove eight out of 18 cysts from my liver. The largest was the size of a small watermelon. My pain was severe, and I wasn't observant of the medical protocol. After being released for a few days, I was hospitalized again with infections. I lost over 20 pounds in a few weeks.

Enduring the liver cyst removal process helped me to understand the need to rid ourselves of unwanted growths. Now I have empathy.

Questions to Answer:

ↄ Have you had a horrible situation happen to you—one from which healing helped you develop empathy?

ↄ What unwanted "cysts" have grown in your life or work?

Reflection: Focus on the Daybreak

Mark well that God doesn't miss a move you make;
he's aware of every step you take.
The shadow of your sin will overtake you;
you'll find yourself stumbling all over yourself in the dark.

Proverbs 5:21-22 (The Message)

God sees all, knows all. In the book of Genesis, Abel tried to hide his murder of Cain. It didn't work. Jonah tried to run away from God—there was nowhere to hide.

I must focus on the daybreak. The sun comes up every morning, and God shines on me like its wonderful light and warmth. His mercies are new every morning. When my life seems like the darkest night, when the shadows overwhelm me, I can focus on the daybreak and know that his mercy, strength, and guidance are near.

In the long, dark, night of the soul, my mind wanders toward things that concern me. I wonder if my child can manage some of the trials. Items of worry seem to scurry out from under everything. But the night is not forever.

night is not forever

Joy comes in the morning. None of my problems can hide from God. Nothing in my child's life is unfixable. I place all my trust in the Lord.

Joy comes in the morning

Questions to Answer:

⊃ Describe a circumstance in your life that is too big for you to handle.

⊃ What steps do you take to push through?

⊃ What lessons have you learned?

Reflection: Look at the Gift Inside

Have you ever received a beautifully gift-wrapped package with lovely bows, flawless handwriting on the gift card, and all the promise of something wonderful inside—but the gift couldn't live up to the packaging?

Have you ever received a wonderful gift in a grocery sack?

You can't tell a book by its cover or a gift by its wrapping. Ignore the bells and whistles, the trappings, the pretty paper, and look only at the gift itself.

One of my best friends gave me some wise advice as I went through one of the most tragic times of my life.

- ⊃ Work on me, rather than worry about others.
- ⊃ Believe God will help me through this.
- ⊃ Be thankful for the gift. There's always a gift, always in plain sight.
- ⊃ Realize this situation is not about me. God is up to something bigger.

I had a situation when my heart broke. The pain was deep until I literally became ill and nauseated. Yet somehow, I focused on the sky through the window; the sun breaking through a cloud; the music of the birds and the wind—and the pain inside seemed to subside. I felt His strength and His grace by looking outside myself.

Over time, God shifted my focus, and though my heart still aches, I celebrate life.

Questions to Answer:

- ⊃ How do you make it through difficult situations?
- ⊃ What do you focus on that will give you hope?

Reflection: Pain and Wisdom

Bobby Kennedy quoted one of his favorite poets, Aeschylus, as he consoled the people after the assassination of Rev. Dr. Martin Luther King.

He who learns must suffer. And even in our sleep, pain that cannot forget, falls drop by drop upon the heart, and in our own despair, against our will, comes wisdom to us by the awful grace of God.

Aeschylus

Why is it that pain teaches us better than any other lesson in life? C. S. Lewis said, "God whispers to us in our pleasures, speaks in our conscience but shouts in our pains: it is his megaphone to rouse a deaf world."

> Why is it that pain teaches us better than any other lesson in life?

When we have life just where we want it; when everything is going our way; when every day is like an endless blessing—it's then that we grow deaf to God's voice, whether we realize it or not. We're too busy enjoying ourselves. That's when God picks up the megaphone called pain and breaks through all that dangerous insulation.

It hurts, but we hear. We learn. We grow. Believe it or not, pain is one of God's greatest gifts. Without it, there would be no wisdom.

Questions to Answer:

- Discuss how a painful time in your life shaped you for the better?
- How did you grow, and what steps are you taking now?

Reflection: Heavy

Sometimes, life is too heavy to bear. You need not bear it alone; look to God. He is never closer than when you're at your wit's end. He is never more available than when you need a friend. When you come to the end of yourself, you'll find you're at the beginning of his wisdom.

Are you tired? Worn out? Burned out on religion? Come to me. Get away with me and you'll recover your life. I'll show you how to take a real rest. Walk with me and work with me—watch how I do it. Learn the unforced rhythms of grace. I won't lay anything heavy or ill-fitting on you. Keep company with me and you'll learn to live freely and lightly.

Matthew 11:28

Life is hard work, but what God offers is rest for your soul. Have you found that rest lately? Are there people in your life who will help you realize you're at your limit, and it's time to slow down?

Also, who is there in your life who needs a gentle word about being overstressed? What can you do to help?

Questions to Answer:

⊃ List five steps you take to lighten up.
⊃ Have you ever drawn closer to God when times were tough? What happened?
⊃ Do you need rest for your soul right now?

Reflection: Don't Be Scared

Eagles quarterback, Nick Foles, helped lead Philadelphia to an improbable first Super Bowl title after taking over for injured quarterback Carson Wentz in the final weeks of the season. He went from obscure bench-sitter to champion on the world's biggest stage.

Foles said, "I think the big thing is, don't be afraid to fail. In our society today, with Instagram and Twitter, it's a highlight. It's all the good things. When you look at it, you have a bad day, you think your life isn't as good, you're failing."

We measure ourselves against the happy-talk on social media and feel like we're missing out. But if we're struggling, we're actually to be envied! We're the ones growing. We're the ones building character.

Without a little failure, a little humbling, where would you be in life?

Without a little failure, a little humbling, where would you be in life? Foles said, "I wouldn't be up here if I hadn't fallen thousands of times, made mistakes."

Nick Foles found the super-power of humility. He knows his weaknesses, and he turns them to strengths by navigating through with his faith. He embraces the struggles as opportunities to become better today than he was tomorrow.

Even youths grow tired and weary,
and young men stumble and fall;
but those who hope in the LORD
will renew their strength.
They will soar on wings like eagles;
they will run and not grow weary,
they will walk and not be faint.

Isaiah 40:30-31

Questions to Answer:

- Describe a stumble that became a leap—a time when good came from failure.
- What do you fear and how do you plan to face the fear?

Reflection: Springtime

One winter, we had over 25 snow days and record low temperatures. Life has its own winter storms. Sometimes, we feel the brutality of events that have us hoping for the warmth and beauty of the spring season.

Today is the birthday of one of my favorite cousins: Valerie Brown Traore. She and her four siblings began their lives in that kind of "storm": harsh conditions, few resources for the "warmth" we need. Many evenings, Val went to bed hungry. She and her siblings lacked many basic requirements for healthy living. Val's mom passed away when she was only eight, and her father was an inconsistent figure in her life.

Val and her siblings were taken in by our grandmother, Lottie Mama. This was a wonderful turning point in their lives, no less than a dramatic rescue from the storm that was all they knew.

> This was a wonderful turning point in their lives, no less than a dramatic rescue from the storm that was all they knew.

God ordained that she would be born on the first day of spring, a time of hope. Val, as former CEO of the Foodbank of South Jersey, has dedicated her life to ensuring that families never go without food. She is nationally recognized for helping those who need help the most. Now she is an entrepreneur and starting her second act.

In honor of the end of a record harsh winter and the beginning of spring, I salute Val for being generous and fulfilling her life purpose: ensuring that our children and their families experience the warm, hopeful majesty of life's springtime.

1. Live your purpose in life—God made you as his masterpiece. (Ephesians 2:10)
2. Never, never give up. (2 Corinthians 4:16-18)
3. Keep working hard because sooner or later, you'll break through.
4. Never stop believing you can and will *soar*.
5. Celebrate successes large and small.

Questions to Answer:

- How do you "keep warm" in the winter blast of life?
- What are you doing to help others who need to come in from the cold?
- Commit to three acts of kindness that will help others.

Your Mission Statement

Now that you've almost completed this book and addressed the questions on each page, it's time to develop your own mission statement.

Congratulations on making it to this page! This is the section that could become a positive turning point in your life.

Why would you do that? Because every individual and every group needs one. A mission statement is a short, well-organized and thought out expression of your *why*. What is the great goal that organizes your existence on this planet? What's the focus that keeps you from moving in aimless directions?

> *A mission statement is a short, well-organized and thought out expression of your why.*

Throughout this book, the cardinal icon has accompanied certain questions. Review the answers you gave to those questions. Then visit www.carlamaxwellray.com/missionstatement for a series of questions to help you write your very own mission statement. You'll find you've already worked toward the creation of your mission statement.

When you complete your statement, print it, even post it for all to see. Get moving toward it and *hold yourself accountable.*

Share a copy of your mission on our Carla Maxwell Ray Facebook page.

God bless you as you become fiscally secure and experience God's purpose for your life.

you now have the tools to soar and flourish

Now that you have a mission statement and these five pillars of a First Class life, you now have the tools to soar and flourish. Remember:

- ⊃ **Be Disciplined**
- ⊃ **Be a Masterpiece**
- ⊃ **Be Radically Generous**
- ⊃ **Be Diligent**
- ⊃ **Be Resilient**

Review your answers and give them a deadline for completion. My recommendation is that you pick one or two action sets from each Pillar to implement monthly. Some will take time, like budgeting; others are a mindset or attitude shift-like focus. My prayer is that you live a First Class Life!

Guidepost Scriptures

U se these scriptures to help you elevate your standard of living and to help sustain your commitment to a better way of living

1 Chronicles 29:1-*11-12. Leaders first. Everything is yours, Lord!

1 Corinthians 3:6 I have planted, Apollos watered; but God gave the increase.

2 Corinthians 8-9. Generosity chapters.

***2 Corinthians 9:7-11.** Because of your generosity, your lives will be enriched.

2 Kings 4. God replenishes. He multiplies.

2 Samuel 24:24. I will not offer to God that which costs me nothing.

Ephesians 3:20. What do you imagine?

Ezra 8:34. Everything was counted, weighted and recorded.

Luke 14:33. Forsake all.

Luke 16:11. If you cannot be trusted with worldly riches, then who will trust you with true riches?

Habakkuk 2:3. Make the vision plain.

Isaiah 43:19. Our collaboration with God's plan.

Proverbs 24:27. Plan and prepare before launching.

John 3:16. For God so loved the world that He gave his only Son.

Haggai 2:8. Silver & gold

Matthew 10:8. Freely ye have received, freely give

Isaiah 40:21-24. Do you not know? Have you not heard...He merely blows on them & they wither.

Proverbs 29:18. Where there is no revelation, the people cast off restraint; But happy is he who keeps the law.

Luke 18. New members; promise of restoration.

Mark 4:20. Seed growth.

Matthew 14:13-21. Feeding the 5,000.

Matthew 6:19-21. Do not store up treasures. Where is your heart?

Matthew 6:33. Don't worry about it!

Matthew 7:7. "Ask & it will be given."

Psalm 1. "Like a tree planted by the river."

Romans 8:28. All things happen for the good of those that love God.

I Thessalonians 1:2. I thank God for you.

Made in the
USA
Lexington, KY